ALIVE.
AGAIN.

*My Journey from Attorney
to Redemption… in Prison*

Andreea Parc

the three
tomatoes

The Three Tomatoes Book Publishing

Published December 2023
ISBN: 979-8-9891962-1-0
Library of Congress Control Number: 2023921673

For information address:
The Three Tomatoes Book Publishing
6 Soundview Rd.
Glen Cove, NY 11542

Cover design: David Dexter
Interior design: Susan Herbst
Author Photo: Demetriad Studios

Authorization was obtained for the names of people and recipes mentioned in this book. The names of those mentioned without authorization have been changed to protect their privacy.

PRAISE FOR ALIVE. AGAIN.

"This book is incredibly inspiring, offering a fresh perspective on the loss of everything — freedom, dignity, and identity — and the profound transformation required to rediscover one's true self."

~Leonard D. DeCarmine, International bestselling author of *1% More: The Hidden Force to Creating Extraordinary Results in Life And Business*

"Andreea's journey is a testament to the human spirit. Her transformation into and out of prison is awe-inspiring and her unwavering positivity and relentless determination prove that we all have the power to rebound and emerge stronger, not only for personal success but also for the betterment of others."

~Orin Wolf, Broadway Producer

DEDICATION

I dedicate this book to my fellow inmates who helped me know myself and understand human nature, who fed and loved me unconditionally throughout this ordeal. They helped me see the real beauty of life, the strength of human nature, and the soul connection we all share. I love them all.

TABLE OF CONTENTS

FORWARD

I have been an attorney for some 50 years, virtually all of those years having been engaged in the practice of criminal law, either as a federal prosecutor or, on the other side of the courtroom, defending my clients who were accused of crimes. After all those decades and countless cases, I believed I knew all there was to know about the practice of criminal law in the federal courts of the United States. Adreea Parc, in her startlingly personal memoir, *Alive Again, My Journey from Attorney to Redemption… in Prison* has proven me wrong.

What Andreea has done is nothing short of astounding! In her narrative she discusses her arrival from Romania, her rise to the heights of her practice as an immigration lawyer and her misguided choices that led to her indictment, conviction after trial and incarceration. However, and far more importantly, she details how she found her true self in, of all places, federal prison. With excruciating detail, she shares her experiences of love and hate, kindness and cruelty and the gratuitous inhumanity that is suffered by all inmates. Never bitter, Andreea's writing will make you laugh and cry as she encounters obstacle after obstacle to her growth which she is determined to overcome. There can be no doubt that she has become a different and better person—not because of her experience but despite it.

When the lawyering, judging, and sentencing are done, Andreea tells us what really happens to those convicted and incarcerated, something that so few of us think about or know. In our American society where, as she so clearly demonstrates, we suffer from the scourge of mass incarceration, hers is a primer on how we might begin dealing with this issue more effectively and intelligently. I simply do not know anyone...judge, prosecutor, or defender and all concerned citizens...who would not profit from reading Andreea's story.

~ Ronald G. Russo, Esq.

PREFACE

AT THE AGE OF TWENTY-TWO, following my graduation from law school, I left my home in Bucharest, Romania, and embarked on a journey of self-discovery that led me to the United States. Ending up in prison twenty years later, for three years, was not part of the plan.

In the spring of 2018, I was indicted on charges of asylum fraud. The week before Thanksgiving I was found guilty in a jury trial and placed in detention in a Manhattan maximum security holding facility called Metropolitan Correctional Center (MCC) while awaiting sentencing. Yes, the same MCC where El Chapo was housed during his trial and where Jeffery Epstein committed suicide. Eight long months later, I was sentenced and sent to Federal Correctional Institute (FCI), Danbury, aka the "Cupcake Camp." I was still incarcerated when the pandemic hit. I spent nineteen days in solitary confinement, in a windowless room, only because I was exposed to someone who allegedly had COVID. When I came down with COVID I spent another fourteen days in solitary confinement.

How did I go from being a successful attorney with my own practice in New York City, with a good life and a beautiful daughter to losing everything and going to prison...just like that?

I faced a pivotal period in my life where chronic stress and pressure dictated my actions, resulting in professional setbacks and personal struggles. While achieving notable success, I still felt a profound emptiness and a sense of stagnation. I was deep down in a bottomless pit, where it was dark, and it hurt.

My transformation began in the most unlikely of places: alone in a windowless cell in a federal prison. Surrounded by seemingly insurmountable challenges, I experienced a profound shift in perspective and found an unexpected sense of liberation and inner peace. Through this journey of powerlessness, I gained invaluable insights into control, power, and surrendering to a higher purpose.

By sharing my story and transformation, it is my hope that others struggling to regain control of their lives, no matter what their situation is, will be encouraged to embrace a peaceful state of mind that truly sets them free.

INTRODUCTION

THE TERM *PRISON* REFERS TO a state of physical and mental confinement or captivity.

The idea of prison can be overwhelming, with its association to confinement and loss of freedom. It serves as a severe punishment for those who have committed serious crimes, and life inside is a monotonous cycle where one's every move is dictated by someone else. The food is unrecognizable, and the only hope is to stay busy with tedious labor. There is no independence or autonomy here, only regret for past decisions. With little interaction with other prisoners, each day is a struggle to survive, as one's release is dependent on factors beyond one's control.

Prison, however, represents more than just a physical space; it symbolizes restraint, isolation, and punishment, as well. It represents the darkest corners of human action and its consequences. Inmates are surrounded by brick walls but also stigma, shame, and regret. With every passing day, freedom becomes nothing more than a distant dream, a memory that fades away.

The walls and emotions that exist beyond physical confinement are a state of mind. Prison represents more than just physical captivity; it also enslaves the mind. This mental state is something many of us create for ourselves, even when we are comfortable and safe at home. On the other hand, some may be physically imprisoned and find peace.

Living in prison often means limited bathroom time, space, and mirrors, minimal skin, hair, and makeup care, sleeping in open quarters with little privacy; wearing the same drab attire, and feeling disheveled and uncared-for. This lack of freedom, rights, agency, and access to essential self-care products takes a toll on prisoners' well-being and drains their spirits. Communication with loved ones is also heavily restricted. Women are particularly vulnerable to the effects of having so little autonomy. Food is usually the only comfort available, as well as companionship from fellow inmates.

In prison, we are all pretty much the same, regardless of language, background, education, socioeconomic status, age, skin color, or body type. The shared experience of forced surrender and humility unites us in humanity when we suffer together. The social constructs that usually divide us become less critical. It is funny that one needs to get to prison to realize that we are all in this life together and the same.

During the most challenging and difficult period of my life, the kindness and unconditional love I received from strangers who were also suffering makes me look back on those times with a sense of nostalgia. It's strange to think that anyone could feel nostalgic about their time in prison, but that's how impactful those acts of kindness were on me.

Despite language and cultural barriers, we found moments of laughter and fun involving food preparation, cooking, and eating. After all, happiness is a choice.

In prison, some people say there are no friends, but I made some wonderful friendships at a soul level that will last a lifetime.

People respond differently to the specter of prison. Ultimately, it doesn't matter why they are in prison, how they got there, what they look like, or how they feel. What matters is how we choose to react to all those things. We can do nothing about our own minds except control how we play the mental game. Our mind is our best friend or worst enemy, and we can choose which one we want to be.

For many, prison exists as a far-off realm reserved for punishing criminals. Society often segregates individuals into categories of "good" and "bad" without considering the circumstances that may have led the latter to their actions—whether it be hunger, desperation, or mental illness. It begs the question: Have the "good" ever pondered how they would behave in the same situation as the "bad?"

Some people have been imprisoned or jailed all their lives, stigmatized from childhood because their parents or whole families were imprisoned. Everywhere they turn, they encounter conditions that could lead to a similar fate, and they are pushed down a similar path, sometimes unwittingly, sometimes consciously. Many others find themselves in prison unexpectedly for a variety of reasons.

Our self-perception and world view shapes our behaviors, beliefs, and limitations. In the end, we are all equal, and we determine our fate by our actions and choices. To navigate life without acknowledging our inherent flaws and virtues will lead to unhappiness.

It is a sobering thought to think that only 4.25 percent of the world's population lives in the US, but shockingly 20 percent of the world's prisoners are here. The US has become a worldwide leader for having the highest incarceration rate with one alarming statistic: 80 percent of women who are incarcerated are mothers and primary caregivers for their families. The consequences of imprisonment not only take its toll on the person serving time but also on their families back home, which can adversely impact relationships.

Furthermore, not many people know that slavery was banned in the US, except for "the duly convicted." According to the 13th Amendment of the US Constitution slavery remains legal as a punishment. When a case from 1871, Ruffin v. Commonwealth, became law, which is still in effect to this day, it declared that "incarcerated people were legally indistinguishable from enslaved people" and they are "slaves of the state."

Being imprisoned for a certain duration can disturb a person's behavior but also creates new opportunities for growth. It can serve as a lesson, promoting positive alterations. Acknowledging one's involvement in the events leading up to the imprisonment and comprehending them are essential to facilitating transformation. In the journey toward self-improvement being receptive to changing attitudes and taking control of one's own destiny are also imperative factors.

As human beings, our initial instinct is to shift the blame onto others when we make mistakes. We tend to fixate on the negative consequences that follow and try to avoid facing them. However, we tend to ignore the potential for growth and development that these experiences can bring, often resulting in positive transformations.

Based on my three-year observation of individuals in prison, I can confirm that their actions and attitudes while incarcerated are heavily influenced by their mental state, personal beliefs, and societal views.

While in prison, I heard many devastating stories of innocent women taking the hit for someone else. When I listened to their stories, I realized many of these women got into trouble protecting someone they loved. Or while they were being used by someone who loved them—a partner or a child or a parent.

In prison life, both prayer and food hold significant importance. The act of preparing and enjoying meals provides a much-needed break from the harsh and demoralizing reality faced by inmates. For some, prison offers a respite from abusive partners or crime-ridden neighborhoods, while for others, it's a traumatic experience. However, adapting to this new way of life is crucial for survival, and women tend to excel at it due to their protective nature.

When people—especially women—are crushed, when they hit rock bottom, when they are stripped of everything, forced to leave their children, families, and loved ones behind, food is one of the few sources of comfort, one of the few ways to feed not only the body but more importantly the soul.

As with the kitchen at home, cooking in prison brings people together, releases tension, encourages bonding and even friendship, and gives people a reason to keep going.

Throughout history, women have been known to create recipes from meager ingredients and limited resources in order to sustain their families. This ability to provide nourishment and sustenance is an inherent trait of women, who have always been the primary care-givers and life-givers. Women's role as food providers has been vital to the survival of humankind, and it continues to be so even today.

Food is life, even in prison, just like everywhere else on Earth. It binds people, creates friendships, generates laughter, and inspires ingenuity. It provides a creative outlet. Even when women are at their lowest point, food lets them express their inherent nurturing qualities—the desire to entertain, care for, feed, and bring joy to others.

Throughout my story, you will meet many of the women who sustained me and each other in many ways, including with food. Coming together to create and share meals was life-sustaining. To honor them, I have included many of their creative recipes through-out the pages of this book.

The insights shared in this book are applicable to all, regardless of whether we find ourselves in a physical or mental prison. I delve into my method for mastering the mental game of prison, regardless of what kind it is. I draw upon real-life instances to illustrate my approach, which centers on five key components: willingness, awareness, intent, determination, and action.

Life can be challenging, despite its seemingly simple design. It's our own minds that complicate things, and our ability to embrace a peaceful state of mind that truly sets us free. Prison is a mental game.

PART I

MCC
(Metropolitan Correctional Center)

Property of BOP

Chapter 1

HOW I GOT TO MCC
(Metropolitan Correctional Center)

"GO DIRECTLY TO JAIL. Do not pass go, do not collect $200."

Mistakes and bad judgment, stemming from the absence of a well-defined operational system, as well as my inadvertent disregard for established office practices and other external factors that I once deemed coincidental, culminated in a series of unfavorable outcomes. The question that lingered was whether these events were mere coincidences or direct consequences of my actions, or lack thereof?

At that point in time, one would consider what happened a disaster, a nightmare. I certainly did! A successful practicing attorney with my own general practice in New York, with a good life to lose everything and go to prison ... overnight!

In the spring of 2018, I was indicted on charges of asylum fraud. I was offered a plea agreement. These charges resulted from the immigration portion of my practice. I acknowledged I made mistakes and perpetuated some practices that weren't quite kosher to streamline the business, but the punishment I got was way too harsh for the crime.

At least that is what I thought, not knowing that I would end up with two and half more time than what the government offered me initially just because I chose trial instead of plea.

Go figure!

I refused the plea, truly believing I was not guilty of the crime charged and having a blind trust in the American legal system. My ignorance pushed me to ask for a trial instead of getting myself educated with the reality of the criminal legal system in this country. I have never practiced criminal law or had anything to do with this area of law or lifestyle.

I should have known better or at least got educated. In Romanian we have a saying and I remember my family using it a lot *"Prostia si domnia se plateste"* — "Stupidity and show-off has a price."

I took out an equity loan on my already mortgaged apartment and hired two sets of attorneys. As you can see, I continued in my less-than-bright ignorance with all my decisions and paid through the nose.

I looked so put together and sure of myself that nobody dared to even start to tell me how screwed up I was in my actions. I think I was stupid and ignorant, both at the same time, because the stupid have the knowledge but refuse to use it, and the ignorant lack the knowledge and understanding. It was simply my inflated ego.

The one crucial piece of information that I had access to but totally ran away from facing is the percentage of cases in the federal criminal justice system. Pew Research Center gives us the numbers. "Nearly 80,000 people were defendants in federal criminal cases in fiscal 2018, but just 2% of them went to trial. The overwhelming majority (90%) pleaded guilty instead, while the remaining 8% had their cases dismissed, according to a Pew Research Center analysis of data collected by the federal judiciary. Most defendants who did go to trial, meanwhile, were found guilty, either by a jury or judge.

As trials have become rarer, guilty pleas have become more common. Experts have offered a range of explanations for the long decline in criminal trials. Among the most common is what critics refer to as the "trial penalty": Individuals who choose to exercise their constitutional right to trial can face much higher sentences if they invoke the right to trial and lose, according to a 2019 report by the National Association of Criminal Defense Lawyers."

To make the long story short, the government added another charge that carried a mandatory minimum, as punishment for wanting a trial, and after a two-week trial I was, of course—you guessed— found guilty on all counts. That was asylum fraud, false statements, and identity theft that carries a mandatory minimum of twenty-four months. Besides, attorneys are held to a higher standard than the rest of the people, due to their profession.

Now, I have a double citizenship, US and Romanian. Because the judge and the government were already pissed at me for the trial, they had to stick it to me even harder.

Why?

Because they can!

Hence, after the verdict was read, the judge revoked my bail and ordered the marshals to take me into custody. Custody, come to find out, was in MCC located at 150 Park Row, a holding facility for pending trials and sentencing in lower Manhattan that was connected with the federal court by tunnels and dungeons. In 2020 due to various incidents and disrepair, the MCC building was temporarily closed.

So, attorney by day and inmate by night, I was a flight risk in the eyes of the judge and required restraint.

Had I pleaded guilty to the government offer of two years, I would have been given a date to surrender directly to Danbury and ultimately do about eighteen months or less, and never go through the trauma suffered in MCC for eight months.

But, as we all know, everything happens for a reason. I've learned how to play the "mental game of prison," and I was shocked out of my life and found my peace. To be fair, without MCC, I probably never would have written this book about so many out-of-this-world experiences. Every decision is a lesson, and every failure is a step closer to success. We all are where we have to be. These kinds of experiences are the real opportunities to make a change to better our lives.

I created the situation, and now I had to find ways to survive, evolve out of the situation, and use it to help others!

Chapter 2

THE JOURNEY

IT HAPPENED THAT A FEW years back, I went to see a client who was detained in MCC and remained traumatized by the experience. It was the very first prison I had entered ever, as an attorney. The sounds of the locked metal doors, the wired / fenced-up elevators, the darkness, the indescribable repugnant smell, the cold, the restrictions, and the scary and intimidating guards... I was more afraid of the guards than the inmates. I remember I was so uncomfortable that I could not wait to get out of the building.

When I say restrictions, I refer to the fact that attorneys are not allowed to have anything on them. Even the papers are all inspected. I removed my overcoat, jewelry, and shoes, and passed through the security gate. I had to place everything but the shoes in a locker they provide for attorneys. I only had a little folder with a couple of papers for the client to sign. The guard inspected those, but before I would be let inside, he measured me from top to bottom and said, "Wait here!" as he walked away to speak with another officer on the other side of the room. I remember I was wearing a black pantsuit, nothing special, the suit that I usually wore going to court or to the office.

He came back and told me that I could not go in because my pants were too tight and were not proper attire. He was so scary looking that I refused to attempt any conversation with him. I took my stuff from the locker and off I was to find something "decent" to wear. I was able to find a black dress at a store nearby that I wore on top of the pants and returned to try again to enter MCC.

Well, now was a totally different story! I was in the custody of the marshals. They took all my clothes and jewelry, asked me if I wanted to donate them since I wouldn't need them for a few good years, and gave me crap.

Shit! I am here to stay this time!

Weird questions at intake and medical, handcuffs and shackles, tied together around the waist with a thick chain and lock. Stripped and squatted, which means checked in all the bodily orifices for concealed contraband, changed out of my clothing to some sort of huge cover-ups, used underwear, and plastic shoes. *Am I in a horror movie?!*

I was rushed upstairs because it was 9:00 p.m. and I had to be in for the count. I was shoved in an elevator facing the metal in the back corner. The same terrifying elevator. All metal, dark, cold, and stinky. The elevator door opened, and I heard yelling. I didn't know what floor it was. As an inmate in an elevator you have to face the wall, basically with the back toward the door and the officers—the one operating the elevator and the accompanying officer. Officers commanded me to exit. When I turned to exit the elevator, I saw a young girl dressed in gray sweatpants and top, pulling two huge black garbage bags and an officer yelling at her to move faster. She was yelling back about her inability to do so.

Then the officer stopped and addressed me: "OK with a top?"

I shrugged my shoulders. I didn't understand what he meant, nor did I care at that point.

Chapter 3

BEAST OR GUARDIAN ANGEL?

THE OFFICER TOOK ME IN through a dark hallway with three locked metal doors, which meant unlocking one would require locking the other one behind. The garbage girl was behind me, still yelling, and the officer in front was doing the same.

Once we got in the unit, he unlocked the first cell door on the left of the entrance and tried to push me in. A girl from the inside started yelling and pulling the door so the officer could not open it. The girl was cursing and yelling at the top of her lungs and the officer was responding in the same manner. *Would this be the normal way of communication in this place?* I wondered silently.

She nearly got into a fistfight with the officer. I was terrified. It was surreal. I was eventually let into the cell. I stood in a corner speechless, clutching my belongings—the bedroll, that is. *How will I survive being locked in this tiny cell with this wild beast?*

It was a windowless eight foot by ten-foot room with a metal bunk bed, one metal locker, one open toilet, a small sink, a small table stuck to the wall, and two plastic chairs.

After my cellmate's storm had passed, the first question to me was, "Do you speak English?" We started to talk.

It turned out her rage came from an earlier dispute that had nothing to do with me. Karen (not her real name), who had been in MCC for eight months already, gave me a quick rundown of the unit, schedules, people—both inmates and officers—meals, medications, computers, phones etcetera. Since I didn't have anything but the uniform and used (yes, used) underwear I was given at intake, Karen gave me almost everything I needed. A pair of new underwear, socks, sweatshirt and pants, a plastic fork, and a plastic spoon. Plastic knives are not allowed in maximum security holding facilities like MCC; plastic forks were out of stock in the commissary, so this was kind of a prized possession to have.

For months that plastic fork was indeed my prized possession, until it broke trying to mash a potato. For the next couple of months, I ate everything with the plastic spoon until the commissary restocked. On the commissary sheet it was listed as flatware. At that time, they were out of stock. Flatware or utensils came as a pack of yellow plastic spoon, teaspoon, and fork at the price of one dollar.

Karen also gave me one of her plastic mugs, Whirley coffee mug as listed on the commissary sheet, which was out of stock as well most of the time. She asked me if I had eaten. She opened her locker and offered me whatever she had. It was one of the most loving moments I had experienced from a stranger in my life. Spontaneously, completely unprompted, she opened her heart and soul to help as much as she could.

Karen was a twenty-eight-year-old from Bayside, Queens. She had long dark hair and white skin with several piercings where jewelry used to be. Jewelry is not allowed in federal prison. Unfortunately, although from a good middle-class German family, she had a rough upbringing. Ever since she was young, she had been addicted to pills and then drugs. She told me that prison saved her life and that for the past two years, thirty of her friends had died of overdose. She continued to confess how grateful and fortunate she was to be alive because she OD'd twice already. For somebody who didn't know anybody who used drugs, Karen's stories were beyond belief. Very soon, that night I realized how blessed I was with my life and that my problem was not that serious. It was not life-and-death.

The funniest part of the night was when she had to teach me how to get to the top bunk. Then I realized what the officer asked me when I got in.

But wait, before I could go to sleep, we realized there was no mattress for the metal blade upper bunk. We were at the mercy of the angry officer from earlier. Karen started banging on the metal door yelling for the officer to bring me a mattress. After a while we heard the door unlocking.

"That's all I could find," he said, as he shoved a skinny plastic mattress into the cell. "You can ask for a regular one tomorrow," he continued.

It was a thin and what used to be a green color, all dirty and ripped and stinky, on top of everything else. Karen explained that these were the mattresses that they give people on suicide watch or in withdrawals. Karen had an extra blanket and helped me wrap the mattress in it. I put the bedsheet they gave me on top. At that point it didn't really matter where I was sleeping if that would even happen.

At the maximum-security holding facilities, intended for people waiting for trial or sentencing, the simple metal bunks do not have ladders. I was grateful that at that point in time I was super skinny due to the stress of the trial, etcetera. With the help of two chairs and Karen hoisting my butt up, I was able to climb into my bed. Eventually I got a new mattress and developed a strategy where I was able to climb up to the top bunk and come down with ease without the use of chairs.

Furthermore, because the main unit was full, Karen's and my cell was in the Special Housing Unit (SHU), a separate area meant for disciplinary inmates, which was smaller with no windows. But it had a shower. We had the only cell with a shower. Which meant I was able to take a shower that night. (Oh bliss.) Karen was kind enough to lend me her toiletries.

The bedroll I was given was a used rolled-up brown bedsheet, along with one small brown towel and two hand towels, the little squares. In the middle I found a mini version of hand soap, two doll-size bottles of shampoo, and a tiny toothbrush. When I say tiny, it was tiny. I believe my teacup poodle's toothbrush was bigger.

For the next few days, I lived on Karen's coffee and cookies. Yet unaccustomed to prison food, I found the meals served in the main line completely inedible. The smell alone made my stomach turn. The commissary purchases were once a week, and this week was closed for the holiday. Remember, it was Thanksgiving! It would not be open until the following week, plus I didn't have any money on my books.

I was told it was a temporary glitch in the "system," and for six days I could not make a phone call, use the computer, or buy anything. Somehow the "system" wasn't informed that I had arrived. My family could not put money on my books. Not only was I a nonentity, but I was also a completely broke nonentity! My attorney came to see me, and he was told I was "not there." Using someone else's phone account was prohibited, but Karen let me use her phone account to call home briefly.

Due to the glitch and because the unit secretary was annoyed out of her mind with my attitude and questions, on the fourth day she allowed me to call my attorney. Yeah, that rule that you see in the movies where inmates are allowed to make a phone call within the first twenty-four hours somehow did not apply to me. That added even more to my frustrations. I was hungry and in shock, and in jail limbo. A practicing attorney by day and an inmate by night. Mind-boggling. Nothing made any sense!

I was registered under my full name at the time: Andreea Dumitru Parcalaboiu. Although I had been divorced for a few years, I had not registered the name change due to all the licenses, certificates, accolades, and business I had on that name. However, the length and difficulty of spelling of my name was the reason for my nonexistence. After several attempts to get it right, one day they took the liberty to completely remove my maiden name, which mainly caused the confusion. So, they gave me a new ID with Andreea Dumitru. Now, I was searchable. The combination of last name and inmate number was appearing on searches and my family could replenish my books.

Early morning, every day of the week, we could hear the inmates' shackle chains dragging on the floor upstairs. Karen told me that we were one floor below intake. All the inmates from the building going to court or being transferred were dragging by above. Initially it was a chilling sound but then I got used to it. Although I am still startled when I hear chains, keys, and doors slamming.

But with every passing day I realized that despite being hungry, and in a very unusual place, I was safe. I was surrounded by kind people who were all in the same boat. We all had a story. United by suffering. We all had made mistakes; we all had made bad decisions. We were all human, fallible, and fabulous.

Chapter 4

LOST IN TRANSLATION

ON MY ARRIVAL AT MCC, Karen gave me all the information I needed to know, including the fact that single blade razors were the only razors allowed. The commissary would sometimes stock the four pack, but they were out at that time. She said that part of the free feminine hygiene products the Bureau of Prisons (BOP) was offering was a single-use blade that could be obtained at the unit secretary. After the incident with the phone and my name, the unit secretary increasingly grew very unfond of me and my entitled requests.

One morning I saw her coming into the unit with her typical striped skinny trousers and dark UGGs, big Gucci handbag and a very unfriendly look on her face. Her face spoke of her unwillingness and unhappiness to be there. Welcome to the unhappy-to-be-here bunch! The difference between us and her was a matter of choice.

I proceeded to knock on her wide-open door just to announce my presence. Between her unfriendly face and prior experiences with her, my state of shock, exhaustion, and hunger at that point caused my English to totally leave me. I was only able to mumble, asking for a blade instead of a razor—translating from Romanian *razor blade*, it only came out *blade*.

Shortly after she told me she didn't have one I heard my name called by a lady officer with a lot of badges hanging around her neck and a writing board in her hand. She invited me into one of the offices and started a round of questions.

"No, I do not want to hurt myself. No, I have never wanted to hurt myself. No, I do not consume drugs and never did. What is this? I already answered these questions at intake," I asked aggravated.

"I was told you asked for a blade, and you have not been eating since you came. I am obligated to follow up with you in case you want to hurt yourself," she said.

I didn't know if I wanted to laugh or cry, although I felt like doing both at the same time.

"Would you eat the food here?" I asked her. "And I need to shave my legs. If that is not a privilege, which I understood is not, I would really appreciate a razor...blade," I continued.

She made some notes on the pad and invited me out of the room. We stopped by the unit secretary's office. She gave me a single-use razor and asked me to bring it back to her after use. Fine, it didn't pay to argue. She came back to check on me for the next two weeks.

***

I have been wearing contact lenses for at least fifteen years. I had a pair of glasses that I used at home. The day of the verdict, when I was held at MCC, I was wearing contact lenses and I advised them at intake as part of the medical examination.

After a few days of wearing the single-use contact lenses, I again went to my very friendly, by now, unit secretary, the same lady described above. I asked her about the procedure for my family to mail in contact lenses to me.

She looked at me as if I had five heads. "In here you are not allowed contact lenses. You can hurt yourself with those. But you can go to medical, get an eye exam, and they will order glasses for you. The wait time is a minimum six months."

Was this a joke? Okay, clearly nothing in here makes any sense!

The chief officer of the medical department seemed like a nice guy. He was only coming in the unit Friday mornings at town hall, which was the weekly meeting of the inmates and staff to address issues. Everybody was there from the warden to every head of department. So, I approached the gentleman and asked him about the procedure. He confirmed that contact lenses are a luxury and not permitted, but he would make an exception and allow my family to mail him my glasses. After he made a thorough inspection, he would give them to me. And that was how ten days later I got my glasses, which were with me for the next almost three years.

Chapter 5

PEEING IN PUBLIC

THE PROCESS OF USING THE toilet without any privacy was very challenging and embarrassing. It took me a while to accept since I cannot say I got used to it. All the cells are made with the purpose of not having any privacy. The rule is for the unit officer to make rounds and look inside each cell every twenty minutes. In the case of the women's unit, usually, a woman officer must do that. Due to the staff shortages, we rarely had a woman as unit officer. However, at any time, the unit officer or any officer can bust into the cell or just look in through the window of the door. The bed always has to be visible from the window due to the counts. The toilet, in most cases, is right by the door. A prison toilet is usually metal, literally open, no seat, no cover. We carved pieces of carton from the toilet paper boxes and made toilet seats and toilet covers. We were not allowed to use them, but hey, it's prison.

Sometimes the toilet had double-purpose as toilet and chair when girls visited or ate in our cell. The worst was when one of us needed to use the toilet. We had to ask the other ones to leave the room. At nighttime, when the other cellmate was sleeping, you could not do anything but use it. Sometimes it was literally out in public.

One embarrassing yet funny story happened one morning around 7:30. Breakfast was over, computer time was over, and people were going into their cells for the 8:00-10:00 a.m. cleaning. During that half hour my then-bunkie was usually watching TV in the common area. That was my "bathroom time." We were in a cell right by the officers' station. Breakfast fresh fruits were kind of the only fresh food we would get, and everybody in the unit knew that I enjoyed every kind of fruit. That morning they served fresh melon slices.

As I was "doing my business," a fellow lady opened my cell door wide to hand me the fruits she got at breakfast. The opened door left me exposed right in front of the officer. The lady didn't know what to do. I signaled her to close the door. Later that day I went to her cell to get the fruits and we laughed about the ridiculousness of the situation.

Chapter 6

Thanksgiving Day, 2018

It's good to have attorney friends, especially on Thanksgiving Day. Attorneys are allowed in prisons at any time. A good friend of mine, who was in even more shock than me over what happened, visited and spent a big part of that Thanksgiving with me. The visiting rooms were freezing cold, even colder than the female unit and the rest of the building. A/C was blasting all the time and the thick brick walls were radiating cold. Although I was blue from the cold and wearing scraps of clothing as the uniform, I was happy to see a familiar, friendly face.

When I went back to the unit, devastated, heartbroken, and cold, Karen surprised me with food she saved for me from lunch. It was turkey, some canned greens, and mashed potato in a plastic tray with another plastic tray on top. I could not eat a lot, but I was so grateful to have something to eat.

The meal schedule at MCC, and prisons in general, is: breakfast at 6:30 a.m., lunch at 11:00 a.m., and dinner served after the 4:00 p.m. count, which at MCC was at 5:00 p.m.

On holidays, a big lunch is served and, depending on the holiday, is something specific. Along with lunch, inmates receive a brown paper bag containing two hard-boiled eggs, two slices of white Wonder Bread and either jam or peanut butter, as dinner. There is no other dinner served on holidays.

I missed lunch while I was meeting with my attorney friend.

If Karen had not saved food for me, I would not have had anything to eat that Thanksgiving Day. So, I had something to be thankful for.

Chapter 7

KOSHER MEALS

HAWWA WAS THE GIRL WHO served the food. She was a young, fluffy, and funny girl. She loved to eat and tell stories. One day she came to me and said that she had been watching me and noticed that I barely eat—like, anything. I had little appetite at MCC and wasn't able to gag down the group meals.

Meals were especially disgusting, except for the once-a-week beef stew, boiled eggs, baked potato, and salad (lettuce only) most of the food was inedible, at least to me. Breakfast was usually some stale cereal and fruits from a can and 1 percent milk. I got up every morning to get the milk and see if they served fresh fruit. Sometimes it was an apple, a banana, or a slice of melon or pineapple.

Lunch, at 11:00 a.m., was something that I was never interested in. Rice, beans, or some unidentified food. That was my time to go to the gym. The entire unit was rushing to the kitchen. I was going the other way to the gym. Equipped with a large sports bottle (plastic) with freshly made tea, my lunchtime at the gym was well spent.

Dinner was again something that I would rarely eat. Some tacos or burrito with unidentified filling, rice, and beans. As I said, I would rarely get something to eat.

Hawwa, who was Muslim, suggested that I apply for the kosher meal. At MCC, it didn't really matter who was what. We were all the same. I told her I am not Jewish. She explained that because the kosher meal was the only special meal available, the chaplain approves it for anyone with a religious or dietary restriction. She even spoke to the chaplain on my behalf, and following a short interview he approved my special meals.

This was another story altogether. I would receive bags of pink salmon, sardines, chicken bologna, V8 juice, dry oatmeal, and some cooked meals. And...fresh fruit, and a delicious omelet on Saturday mornings. Wow, this was luxury!

When I wasn't eating them myself, I was happy to make others happy with them. My kosher meals never went to waste. Thanks to Hawwa I was able to have some kind of edible food every day.

Adjusting to being locked up in a cell with a stranger, with a freestanding toilet next to the bed, given only ten minutes for a phone call a day, having very limited options of food, living with a near total lack of privacy, and without basically every human right is daunting, to say the least. Holidays in prison are especially painful. Holidays are meant to be spent with family and loved ones, meant to share food and fun and stories, meant to be magical. So, I sought to create my own magic.

Most of the white-collar criminals I heard of and met later on in my journey had not been handcuffed or incarcerated before sentencing. They were usually given a date and place to surrender to, at the closest Camp to the place of residence. But until then, they got to be at home. I was just special, I guess. I had to learn my lessons the hard way! I was given the opportunity to win the mental game of prison.

Hawwa's Survival Meals

"Good day! It's me Hawwa Safani, aka tri-state
Dirty Diamond. I hope everybody goes home and prospers in
their life and gives back to humanity!
Enjoy my recipes for MCC Jail Survival Foods. LOL."
xoxoxo Hawwa

Banana Crumble Cake

Ingredients
- bananas (as many as you can get)
- 2 oatmeal cookie
- 1 cup creamer
- 1 milk
- 1-2 donuts

Instructions
1. Crush all the ingredients and place in a bowl.
2. Microwave for 2-4 minutes until thick.

Sushi Roll

Ingredients
- 7 pkg rice
- 2 pkg plain oatmeal
- plastic trash bags big enough for the amount
- seasonings by taste: mayo, mustard, chipotle sauce, jalapeños, Sazón, garlic, salt and pepper, BBQ sauce, lemon pepper
- 2 bar Swiss cheese
- 1 turkey stick Slim Jim
- powdered cheese from the mac and cheese
- 2-4 pkg any fish or meat
- soy sauce

Instructions
1. Microwave rice until fluffed.
2. Roll it out onto trash bags, flip it twice, and tie the ends.
3. Enjoy it with soy sauce or any other sauce!

Pizza Mama Mia!

Ingredients

- soft tortilla shells
- paper plates
- cardboard boxes (to use in the microwave)
- any type of meat (cooked in separate bowls)
- any cheese (crumbled, put on top)
- any sauce
- seasonings

Instructions

1. Set the soft tortilla on paper plates.
2. Add the sauce, meats, cheeses, and seasonings.
3. Place the paper plate on top of the cardboard and cook until cheese is melted.

Chapter 8

PROPERTY OF BOP
AND STAYING SANE

WE WERE TOLD ON A regular basis, "You are the property of BOP," the Federal Bureau of Prisons. My mind could not process how a human being, a US citizen in the United States, in the year of our Lord 2018, could be told he or she or they have been stripped of all rights, and is now the property of the US government. Wow. Let's not forget that prisoners are the "slaves of the state."

The winter jackets that were available to both men and women for outside fresh air time on the roof, mostly for thirty minutes to one hour, had an inscription on the back, *Property of BOP*. They were old and dirty and worn-out. I wondered about the inscription. It's not as if anybody would steal the jackets. Or was it a reminder to the person wearing the jacket that they are property of the BOP?

As part of being property of the BOP, aka slaves, ice, hot water, showers, phone, computer, television, commissary, fresh air, and microwave are privileges. At any moment in time, without any warning, we were locked in the cells without access to any of the above. I advised my family of this rule so they wouldn't worry when I didn't call for hours or even days on end. Visits were a privilege, as well. From my cell window I was able to see the visitors' entrance. I saw my daughter waiting to be allowed in the building for visitation. One time due to a lockdown in the entire building, all the visits were canceled. I saw my daughter walking away crying. The feeling that I could see her, without her seeing me, and not being able to talk to her was unbearable.

And what was even more unbearable was that I had no control over what was happening to me. Anything could happen at any time. That was the beginning of my mastery to the mental game of prison. Being able to control my mind was the ultimate control.

***

My Daily Prison Routine

My determination to keep my mind in check gave me the power to stick to a routine that gave me peace.

Meditation six times a day
Bike one hour (in the gym)
Treadmill one hour (in the gym)
Outside rec one hour (if any)
Reading/Writing
Gratitude journaling
Eating/Socializing
Sleep

Chapter 9

THE FIGHT

MY TIME WITH KAREN IN that room was short-lived. One night, right before the 9:00 p.m. count, the unit was placed in lockdown. I was reading in my bunk when an officer came to our cell to tell us to pack our stuff, we were moving out. Unbeknown to me, some girls got into a fight. As is procedure, the entire unit was put in lockdown, usually for a minimum of twenty-four hours. During lockdown, all inmates are locked in their cells. That meant no using computers, no making phone calls, no having visitors, no taking showers. Some officers were nice enough to let us go to the kitchen area and get hot water for our morning coffee.

During lockdown, my drinking water was tap water from the cell's sink. On a regular basis my drinking water was cooled off hot water or ice mixed with hot water. We were told access to the shower, ice and hot water, watching TV, using the microwave, buying items in the commissary, having visits, access to phone and emails, or using the gym or laundry were privileges not rights. The food was brought to the cell in small plastic trays.

The people who fought were sent to the SHU for at least thirty days. The SHU is basically solitary confinement. The female unit at MCC had only one SHU cell, the one that was occupied by Karen and me. Hence, one of the girls who got into the fight, the one who got injured, was kept at MCC and the other one was already shipped to Metropolitan Detention Center, Brooklyn (MDC). "Shipped," that's right. As a package, not a human. Property of the BOP, remember?

Since we had to move out, this ignited another hysterical screaming episode from Karen. She almost got shipped to the SHU in Brooklyn herself.

I was moved to another cell which, surprisingly, had two windows and a view of the Brooklyn Bridge, of course through the bars. It was right above the waiting area of the visiting entrance. Prime location! Maybe my luck was changing.

The female unit at MCC was formed of ten cells of two people and five cells of three people, one SHU cell, and one suicide watch cell. The maximum occupancy was forty people. The unit also had a gym (with one bike, one treadmill and couple of yoga mats), two common areas with tables and TVs, four computers, four phones, and two showers. There was an open space with counters for cooking where the microwave, hot water dispenser, and ice machine were located that people would call kitchen. A laundry room and a religious room were in the back of the unit.

The space was open for us to use when we were not locked in for counts or lockdowns. We were locked in the cells from 9:30 p.m. until 6:30 a.m. The night counts were at 10:00 p.m., 12:00 a.m., 3:00 a.m., and 5:00 a.m. The counts were done by two officers with flashlights through the secured window of the cell door. Breakfast was served at 6:30 a.m. The computers were open to use from 6:30 a.m. to 7:30 a.m. From 8:00 a.m. to 10:00 a.m. we were in the cells. Two designated inmates were cleaning the hallways and common areas at that time, so we had to stay in. From 10:00 a.m. to 3:30 p.m. we were allowed to be free within the unit, wearing the uniform and institution shoes. At 11:00 a.m. lunch was served.

Once a week we were allowed to do laundry and go out of the unit on the same floor to the library. Also, once or twice a week an officer from recreation would come to get us out on the roof for a maximum of one hour to take fresh air. It was a small, wired square but at least it was fresh air. I was walking around in circles, listening to music on my MP3 player, a very expensive purchase from the commissary. Each song had to be purchased separately. Looking up through the fence and cameras I would see the top of the courts I used to practice in not long ago. It was a very weird feeling to see them from behind the fence. I guess that is the nature of the beast, the purpose of punishment. Again, it was about winning the game of my mind. I would not let anyone win that game.

From 3:30 p.m. to 5:00 p.m. we were locked in again for count. At 5:00 p.m. dinner was served. After the 5:00 p.m. count and on weekends, we were allowed to wear the gray attire instead of the uniform and slides.

Chapter 10

HOOCH, CHRISTMAS, AND NEW YEAR'S

MY NEW BUNKIE, LET'S CALL her Susan, was a funny and very wise Hispanic lady slightly older than me, who told me the entire story behind the fight. Bottom line, a silly argument about nothing, feelings got hurt, then there goes the punch heard round the unit.

During the fight one of the girls fell on her knee on the metal bed and hurt herself. She was the one that stayed at MCC. At search, after they were shipped, the COs (correction officers) also found some homemade punch, aka hooch—an alcoholic drink made from fruits—in the cell, which of course in prison is contraband and illegal.

Susan was grateful that the officers who searched the rooms only took the girls and did not make a big deal out of the hooch, which they confiscated. Otherwise, the entire unit would have gotten into deep trouble. Susan told me that the officers searched only the two respective cells of the girls who got into the fight and not the entire unit.

***

Christmas and New Year

For Christmas 2018, we cleaned our cell thoroughly including the walls. We shifted the energies; we turned the bunk bed around and declared a new beginning. We prayed together until morning and for the first time in my life I felt the Divine presence. I felt protected. I knew I was safe. I knew as bad as the situation seemed it was the best thing that could have happened to me. It was my time for transformation. I was the ugly worm in the cocoon working toward my release as a majestic butterfly.

Locked up with Susan in our "prime location" cell, watching the New Year's Eve fireworks over the Brooklyn Bridge through the bars on the windows, we prayed again and made plans for the future. We made a little platter of nuts and cheeses we bought from the commissary, and we cheered with virgin Bloody Marys made from V8 with pepper. The V8 was a privilege from my kosher meals.

Chapter 11

ENTERTAINMENT

THE WINTER OF 2019 WAS brutal. The building had no heat. The women's unit was on the second floor, the same level as the medical office and the library for the entire population. We were placed in lockdowns only when the girls got into fights, or when they would bring El Chapo (yes, that El Chapo) to medical. He was detained in the same building on the tenth floor. Yes, he had the entire tenth floor for himself. Although he was locked up in a small cell with surveillance 24/7, no one else except officers were allowed on that floor.

When he was taken out of the cell either to be transported to court in Brooklyn or to be brought to medical, the entire building was placed in lockdown. It was quite a show, seeing the elaborate security procedure in place to transport him to and from the court in Brooklyn where he was tried. The entire building was surrounded by police cars, all traffic stopped. From the limited view out our windows, we would follow the caravan of cars as they left the prison and crossed the Brooklyn Bridge.

Susan was very protective of me. She is actually the reason I started writing this book. She forced me to take vitamins, not to get sick, and got some extra bedsheets that we used to cover the windows at nighttime to protect against the wind blowing in, but she especially kept me on schedule with food and eating. My Hispanic big sister. She introduced me to the Hispanic ladies who were cooking all the time. Usually, it was fun, and every night people would gather in the kitchen area and cook, talk, and laugh.

Of course, there was the Spanish TV where all the Spanish-speaking ladies would gather around and always cook. This is how this book was born. *Las mujeres latinas* kept me fed and entertained every day, whether they spoke any English or not. And I don't speak Spanish.

Susan was always gathering with the Hispanic ladies. Although she was born in the US, she has family in the Dominican Republic and Puerto Rico. She always had an interesting and funny story to tell, always with a lesson attached. With her dark hair and light to medium skin, she was very elegant and put together even when we didn't have a lot. She would color her roots with instant coffee for visits and had her hair done.

She would appear at the doorway of our cell and yell, "Andreea, put the book down and go stay with the girls. They cooked, it's good! Just go socialize! Don't be like a library mouse!"

So, I would go, eat something, and actually like it very much. Slowly I started to go to the kitchen with the notebook and write down what they were doing. In the kitchen area at MCC is where this book was born.

Our cell was situated directly above the visitors' entrance, which made it easier for us to see our loved ones and for them to see us before the visitation time. We placed a few colored pieces of paper through the bars, allowing my daughter and Susan's two daughters to easily identify our cell. Before they entered the building, we would wave at each other, serving as a signal that they had arrived. This system helped us be prepared to be called for our visitation time.

We also extended this gesture to help the other girls who didn't have access to a window or a view of the front entrance. By alerting them about their families' arrivals, we ensured that everyone had the opportunity to get ready promptly. The faster we could assemble, the more time we would have to spend with our loved ones during the visitation period, which was a maximum of one hour. For security reasons, they would take us in batches of approximately ten at a time.

So, that winter we were without heat for more than one week at the end of January 2019 when temperatures dipped below twenty degrees Fahrenheit. We slept in every stitch of clothing in our possession, including hats. We were given an extra blanket. We filled our water bottles with hot water to keep warm. The thick walls of the building were emanating cold. We pulled the bunk bed into the middle of the room, away from the wall. We got large garbage bags and taped them to the windows, which we weren't allowed to do, but hey, it's prison and we were in survival mode!

The men detained on the upper floors of the building were outraged by the conditions. We could hear them banging on the walls, bars, and windows.

Sometimes the recreation department brought yarn and knitting needles to the ladies in the unit to make stuffed animals or other projects. It was just to give them something to do, and the final products were not allowed to remain in the unit. The inmates were allowed to mail the projects home or donate them to the recreation area to be given out to the community.

However, when the cold hit, all the yarn was used to make hats, scarves, or gloves. Susan got herself a hat and a scarf and pushed me to talk to Mama Georgia to make me one set, as well.

Mama Georgia was an older woman from Georgia, a country in Eastern Europe, who spoke only Russian and very few English words. All day she was knitting and cooking for the younger Russian-speaking girls. I asked one of them to help me speak with Mama Georgia. She told me she would do it, but she ran out of yarn. I don't know how and from where Susan came up with two skeins. This is how in a couple of days I got a hat and a scarf that I would sleep with. We were not allowed to wear them in the unit or going outside for recreation, but the officers let us wear them in our rooms or at nighttime.

In the winter of 2019, besides being cold, it snowed a few times. One of the most exciting times of the day was when we were going outside on the roof for fresh air. It wasn't a big space, as I said, but enough to walk around. Because there were many more men than women, they had priority to go out. We got only one hour, at most, once or twice a week. A handful of us went outside regularly. It was me, Susan, the Russian-speaking ladies, and couple of other people. That's all!

The officers were nice enough to let us know an hour in advance, so we would have time to dress for the wintertime with all the clothes we had. Only once or twice, when it was really cold, I used the dirty oversize Property of the BOP jacket.

One time after the snow, the recreation officer called to let us know that the roof was closed because of the snow. We were all wearing the institutional shoes, with the slim rubber sole and blue fabric on top. The commissary was out of sneakers. They had nobody to shovel the snow and spread salt.

I was ready to go outside, even barefoot. Santa, one of the Russian speaking ladies, was ready, as well. So, we offered our shoveling services to the recreation officer, just so we could get some fresh air and see the sky. He wasn't too happy that two women would shovel the roof, but he agreed. Santa and I were like kids. Big smiles, rosy cheeks, frozen hands and feet. But who cared? We were outside! Because of our cleaning, we all got to go outside every day that week.

The best part of trying to keep warm was the beef stew turned into beef soup. It was a spicy, hot mix of beef and V8 and noodles. It warmed the body, heart, and soul.

Almost every Monday at dinner we had beef stew. Juicy and tender pieces of meat with carrots and potatoes would go into a big bowl. We would add a pack or two of the ramen beef soup including the noodles sold at the commissary and a couple of cans of my V8 juice. Susan's idea. And hot sauce! Never enough hot sauce! Microwaved to the perfect temperature. So hot and spicy that we would not even feel the cold.

We even had birthday parties that were exceptionally entertaining. We were all contributing to the food cooked with whatever we had. One designated person would cook unless the celebrated birthday was for the cook. From sushi to all kinds of spreads and cakes. Birthdays were an all-day long celebration, except for the counts. We also had the artsy girls who were in charge of the decorations. The recreation officers were nice enough to provide limited supplies but enough for a creative and ingenious person to come up with something quite nice.

One day, Mama Georgia was handcuffed and taken away along with a bowl of some fruits. She was making applesauce, apple juice, or baked apples for dessert. Cells were randomly searched at various times, in addition to the periodic shakedowns. But that day Mama Georgia, who spoke no English, was taken away and brought back a few hours later.

They tested her and the suspiciously hidden-in-plain-sight apples. She was told via an interpreter that she is not allowed to stock up on apples. Well, the truth is that we all kept fruits in our lockers as snacks. This is how we made the delicious fruit salads. And some people—the hooch.

***

The Russian-Speaking Ladies and Their Recipes

"My name is Ketevan. I am sixty-seven years old from Georgia, a country in Eastern Europe. I have been in the US for fifteen years. I am a caregiver and have two children. I like to knit, cook, and play cards." (This is Mama Georgia and I obtained this statement from her with Santa's help)

"My name is Santa. I am forty-two years old from Latvia. I am in the US for four years. I have two children and am an accountant. I like to read, knit, and I like men."

"My name is Eleonora. I am thirty-six years old from Ukraine. I am visiting the US. I have one son at home. I am a dance trainer. My students became world champions three times. I like to study and learn new things and wish to marry Leonardo DiCaprio."

"My name is Liz. I am thirty years old from Ukraine. I have been in the US for four years. I am a gym trainer and studied sports psychology. I like exercising, reading, listening to music, and Black men."

Egg Salad (close to the traditional Soviet New Year salad)
Ingredients
- fried potatoes (main line)
- boiled eggs
- pickles
- peas

- carrots
- corn
- iceberg lettuce
- chicken bologna
- sausage
- mayo
- mustard
- salt and pepper

Instructions
1. Cut all to small pieces and mix together.

Tortilla Wrap

Ingredients
- tortilla
- ketchup
- chicken bologna or sausage
- iceberg lettuce
- boiled egg
- mayo
- mustard
- cheese

Instructions
1. Wrap all ingredients (cut to small pieces) in the tortilla.
2. Microwave for 1 minute.

Baked Apples or Jam and Apple Juice.
This recipe got Mama Georgia in trouble.

Ingredients
- Apples

Instructions
- Put the apples in a box with a lid without water and microwave for 2.5-6 minutes depending on what you want to make.
- For jam, peel the apples and take the seeds out. Mash and add sugar or honey (optional).
- The juice can be enjoyed separately as is or with sugar and ice.

Ketella (Nutella by Ketevan aka Mama Georgia)

Ingredients
- chocolate bar
- creamer
- hot chocolate powder
- milk
- peanut butter

Instructions
1. Break chocolate bar into pieces and put into bowl.
2. Add 3 tablespoons of creamer and 3 tablespoons of hot chocolate powder.
3. Warm one cup of milk in the microwave 45 seconds–1 minute. Add to the bowl on top of the ingredients and mix until melted and creamy. Microwave for 1 min, mix it.
4. Repeat 2 or 3 times. Leave it to cool down.
5. Add the peanut butter 3 tablespoons and mix it vigorously.

Chapter 12

MICROWAVE AND BOWLS

AT DINNER, BEFORE UNLOCKING THE cell doors, people would start yelling through the doors, "Microwave, microwave." It meant that it was the start of the line for cooking. As part of our meager privileges, the unit manager, a very nice and understanding man, made sure we had a microwave. Alas, there was not always peace surrounding that poor microwave. We have been in lockdowns several times due to fights over the microwave. What can you do but laugh about it?

To prevent any future conflicts, we established our own set of guidelines for microwave usage. Initially, we implemented a queue system, assigning specific timings and priorities to each person. However, we made it clear that officers always had top priority, even though they rarely used our microwave since they had one in their office. Nonetheless, there were a few rare instances when their office microwave was out of order.

"Bring your bowls!"

When the serving lady, a fellow inmate, called out "Bring your bowls!" it signaled that either salad or beef stew was being served. For any meal usually we would get trays of food—plastic trays with compartments—but sometimes they would bring hotel pans with either salad, roasted potatoes, or cut fruit. Each of us would line up with our individual bowls to get some.

The line was formed in the hallway along the phones. While the meals were being served the use of the phones was not allowed. One particular officer stood by the phones and if anybody tried to make a phone call, he would bang on the metal side of the phone cover yelling for the person to get off the phone. The experience was so loud and annoying that rarely did anyone try to make a phone call.

Can you guess who the officer was? Right, the yelling one from my first day! It turns out that although he was very loud, he was a responsible and caring person. A former military officer, after an injury he turned to being a correction officer. During the United States federal government shutdown on December 22, 2018, until January 25, 2019 (thirty-five days), which was the longest government shutdown in history, a lot of the officers who are government employees didn't show up for work because they were not paid. The men's units were all in lockdown during this time because there were no officers. This particular officer showed up to work every day, even if he wasn't paid, simply because he cared about us. Because of him we were free in the unit and had no lockdowns.

Chapter 13

CHOCHO AND MY EPIPHANY

AFTER BREAKFAST ON MY FIRST day at MCC, I went to the reading/prayer room. There were very few books that interested me. On top of the bookshelf was a picture of Jesus holding a star. When I looked up, I felt that star shining in my eyes, blinding me for a split second. I turned my head down and when I opened my eyes, right in front of me was a Bible. I have tried several times to read the Bible in Romanian and I could not understand much. What I was reading before the trial were the Psalms. I opened the Bible to a random page and realized that reading it in English makes much more sense.

A few days into my detention, a girl came up to me as I was reading the Bible. "I have a book for you. I see you are reading the Bible. I am sure you will love this one, as well. It's metaphysics." she said. "My name is Chocho."

"Hi, I am Andreea. I don't know what metaphysics is, but I am ready to read the book you are offering me. Thank you," I answered.

She took me to her room and showed me a box full of books. She had several by Emmet Fox, an author I had never heard of. Metaphysics was not my thing.

But in just the first few pages, I was dazzled by a paragraph and read it over and over and over again.

"You could overcome any situation in your life if you choose to raise your consciousness. You can be in prison at this time (*whaaat?*) or in a shelter. But if you choose to raise your consciousness, your life will take a very different turn."

This book was talking to me. And right there, all of a sudden, bam! Everything was clear: I was meant to be there, in a nasty prison cell. I could take this opportunity to make a conscious choice to change my life.

And just like that, for the first time in my life, I was free. A nobody, with nothing, locked in a cell nowhere and in no time, and I finally felt at peace! And it was so good.

Chocho was a twenty-something, tiny, loud, and very funny girl. She spoke perfect English and perfect Spanish. She was always singing, dancing, laughing, telling jokes and stories, and of course cooking. She was born in the Dominican Republic, but by the age of one her family had moved to the US.

Not only did I read that particular book a few times until I almost learned it by heart, but I read all the other books in Chocho's collection. And from there, things started to open up for me. Other books came to me as answers in the order of my questions.

A few months into my stay at MCC she took over the food service from Hawwa. When she had leftovers—fruits, milk, or boiled eggs—she would yell my name from across the kitchen to come get them.

Before I left MCC she came to my cell and gave me *The New Earth* by Eckhart Tolle. She said she found it at the library and that I would love it. Love it? That book was again another stepping stone in my growth.

Chocho organized the Christmas tree for the unit and the thirteen days of Christmas event. I don't know how she did it because we were not allowed to have music in the unit. Every day something was organized. She worked together with the unit manager and the recreation department. Besides the games playing every night, cooking, and listening to music all in the common area between the counts, we had two shows with outside artists who were volunteering at the BOP. It was a very nice way to entertain broken souls.

Chocho's Recipes

"I am Chocho, I am a twenty-eight-year-old originally from the Dominican Republic. I have been in the US for twenty-seven

years. I love to travel, learn new things, cook,
and listen to music."

Mashed Potato with Mackerel by Chocho
for 3 people

Ingredients
- peppers and onions from the meat (main line)
- 8 potatoes (baked, main line)
- milk
- butter
- seasoning (garlic, salt, pepper, adobo, Sazón)
- 3 pc Laughing Cow cheese
- 1 mackerel

Instructions
1. Mash potatoes, add milk, butter, salt, and Laughing Cow.
2. Microwave for 5-6 minutes.
3. Mackerel, adobo, onion, pepper, salt and pepper, and some water, microwave for 6 minutes.

Breaded Chicken by Chocho

Ingredients
- chicken (main line)
- butter
- Ritz crackers
- seasonings

Instructions
1. Season the chicken, crush crackers, dip the chicken into the butter and then the crackers.
2. Microwave to perfection.
3. Enjoy with white rice and beans.

Chocho was especially supportive and clownish during our trips to visiting and back. Every Monday between 5:00-7:00 p.m., family members registered with MCC were allowed to come for visits, for one hour, maximum. No touching or holding hands.

Unfortunately, we rarely ever managed to stay together for even an hour.

Following their arrival and entry through security, by the time they were led to the visiting room our travel from our unit was already underway, aided by two elevators and a squadron of officers as we passed through the male SHO with inmates screaming obscenities at us.

Going back to the unit after our tearful goodbyes was even more unbearable; we were subjected to a full-body search and squat before being taken through the familiar process again.

Chocho was always cracking jokes and making the weekly experience a little easier to manage.

You will find more recipes from the MCC Kitchen and more stories about some of the women who supported each other in the Appendix.

Chapter 14

MY BUNKIE, ROSE

ONE TUESDAY MORNING, EARLY MARCH 2019, right after they unlocked the door, Susan's last name was called by the officers' station. She had her sentencing mid-February, and they usually take about one month to designate and process the transfer to the prison where the sentence is to be served. We knew that all the transfers were done on Tuesdays. Due to security purposes the inmate is not advised when the transfer will take place. Without notice, Susan had fifteen to twenty minutes to get her stuff ready to leave. So, just like that, Susan was gone.

By lunch, I already had a new bunkie, Rose. She was fairly new in the unit and because she wasn't a US citizen, she was held at MCC until sentencing. She was being held in a three-person cell, which was too crowded, so they moved her to my cell.

Rose was Dominican but has been a US resident since she was six years old. She has three children, the oldest an adult, although she was much younger than me, because she had her first son when she was sixteen. She was one of the nicest, kindest, and most caring people I have ever met. My time with her, although short, was precious just because of who she was. Delicate and kind as a rose. She was good friends with Rita, the head cook in the Spanish kitchen. Together we were cooking, talking, and laughing every day, although Rita, who was Mexican, spoke no English. Unfortunately, because both were not US citizens, after sentencing they were either deported or transferred to a prison for noncitizens and we lost contact.

Rose's Recipes

Farina Pudding

Ingredients
- 3 pkt farina
- 2 spoons of creamer
- milk, at least one small carton
- additional sugar if you want

Instructions
1. Microwave in small increments in a large open container. It tends to boil fast and overflow. Depending on the microwave for a total of 5 minutes or until it looks boiled.
2. When done add either jam or chocolate, favorite topping, or enjoy as is!

It took us many, many tries to learn how many seconds to cook it in the microwave. One time we covered the bowl with a lid. It exploded! It took us one hour to clean the microwave and the kitchen. The officer came and asked us jokingly if we are trying to blow up the building.

Tuna con Arroz (Tuna with Rice)

This was Rose's favorite, and she would make it really good.

Ingredients
- Rice
- 1-2 pouches of spicy tuna steak
- spices, sauces

Instructions
1. Cook the rice.
2. Cut the tuna in small pieces, mix with sauces and spices of choice.
3. She added whatever was handy but always some more hot stuff.

Chapter 15

TOILET PAPER CONFISCATED AS CONTRABAND

THE WEEK AFTER SUSAN'S TRANSFER and Rose's move-in, we had a shakedown. I don't know exactly what they were looking for but all of a sudden the unit was flooded with officers yelling at the top of their lungs to drop what we were doing and come out of the rooms into the common area. I was in my bunk working on my sentencing speech and Rose was at work. She took over the laundry position after Marie left. Marie was a big and loud Italian mother. She was always on the move. She worked in the commissary, cleaning, and laundry. When she wasn't working, she was cooking. More on Marie and her recipes in Chapter 31.

I put the notebook down and went to the common area as instructed. I was not worried at all because I knew I didn't have anything that wasn't allowed or illegal. Except for books but those were not a concern to anybody. The limit was seven books for an inmate to have, and I had more than twenty. But again, I wasn't concerned.

After the shakedown was over, another lady and I were called in to see the newly appointed manager.

"Dumitru, what the fuck are you doing with twenty-eight rolls of toilet paper? You know that is contraband!" she asked in an angry tone.

"Ma'am, with all due respect, how can something that is provided to us weekly as a right be contraband?" I replied. "We receive three rolls of toilet paper each week, per person. How much toilet paper can one use?" I could not believe that we were actually talking about toilet paper.

"Dumitru, how do I know you are not selling it?" she said.

I couldn't help myself and started laughing at the ridiculousness of the conversation.

"I am sorry, ma'am, but I can assure you I am not in the business of toilet paper while in here," I replied.

She was "kind enough" not to issue me a ticket for the confiscated contraband, the toilet paper rolls, but she made sure to advise me to give back whatever toilet paper rolls we didn't use by the end of the week.

Of course I agreed, not wanting to further waste my time with the toilet paper subject.

I later discovered the other woman had been summoned for forty individual boxes of Tide she'd purchased from the commissary and stored in her locker. Each room had their turn to do laundry twice a week. Each machine took two laundry bags, so both inmates in a room shared one machine. We all agreed we would do laundry with one machine, combining dark items, gray uniforms, and brown shirts on one day and whites—light gray sweaters, pants, and white socks—on another.

The institution provided Borax as the free detergent, which made laundry smell horrible. However, the commissary sold individual packets of Tide powder. To make our clothes smell a little nicer we all contributed the detergent. For each load, which was the two bags, we used two or three boxes. Although most of us purchased Tide from the commissary, not everyone could afford it, so they used Borax. Each person had a limit of ten boxes that could be purchased from the commissary every week. They confiscated the detergent found in her locker, although she had paid for it, and charged her with having contraband.

Chapter 16

SENTENCING

MCC IS A HOLDING FACILITY for people awaiting trial and sentencing. People don't usually stay at MCC for long unless they have issues with their trial. A lady who was my gym companion was there for five years because she was a codefendant in a large operation with a lot of people involved, but that is not very common.

At my trial, mid-November sentencing was scheduled for the beginning of February. My attorneys kept pushing the date, trying to prepare for a better outcome. So, February turned to March and then April and finally to mid-May. I was fully prepared to let the judge know my current feelings and that I took responsibility for my actions and that ultimately, I was grateful for the opportunity to change.

The sentencing hearing was scheduled for 3:00 p.m. However, I was called at 7:30 a.m. because that is the procedure. They took me up to intake where I went through the strip search and squat procedure, which by then I had accepted. Although I felt humiliated to be completely naked and bent over and had to spread the "cheeks" of my buttocks, and cough two times, to make sure that nothing was concealed up my butt. Then I had to stick my tongue out, up, and down to show there was nothing in my mouth, shake my hair, and show the officer behind both ears, then turn around and show each sole of my foot one by one. Then I was allowed to put my underwear and bra back on, and was given a blue uniform, which was the color of the inmates going to court. I was allowed to keep my gray T-shirt.

When I opened the uniform the female officer gave me, it was a 4X. The pants were falling off and the top reached my knees and my fingertips. I asked the officer if she happened to have a smaller size and the answer was, obviously, *no*.

Okay, what can you do but make fun about it, so I thanked her for giving me the opportunity to wear a dress for sentencing. She didn't get the joke and didn't think it was funny. Because every inmate in this situation is upset and angry, with women especially crying, they could not understand how I could laugh. "What are you smiling about?" was the usual question. They might have thought I was laughing about them. Some situations were so outrageous and ridiculous, without any common sense or meaning, that trying to make sense would be a waste of my energy.

I wasn't going to let anybody else win. And winning the prison game was learning how to control my mind. I didn't know what the government's intention of punishment would ultimately be for me, but at this point it doesn't really matter. I would not let them take over. They had control over my body, but they didn't have control over my mind, the location of all of my thoughts, and the future of my life. Happiness is a choice. I knew everything was temporary and one day I would get to be free and write about it.

They handcuffed and shackled me and then they had a heavy chain that connected the shackles that go around the waist and tie the handcuffs, as well. I had a marshal that closed the handcuffs so tight that my hands went numb. I asked him to loosen them a little bit. He looked at me and said, "You're not going to escape on me, are you?"

"Sir, the chains and clothes are heavier than me, how can I even run?" He was "nice enough" to loosen my handcuffs a little. Then he walked by me marching as if he was in a military parade or accompanying a president of a country!

I was kept in a single cell in the basement of the courthouse the entire day, with the A/C blasting on me. My skin was bluer than the uniform. There is no clock anywhere and I wasn't allowed to have my watch. The only thing I was allowed to have with me was the three pieces of paper I had my speech on. Then, I don't know what time it was, I was transferred to a cell upstairs by the courtroom. I kept my breathing in check, rehearsing my speech, and visualizing myself on top of a majestic mountain with the sun covering me with its warm protective rays.

When the judge was ready for me, another marshal came in to get me. He looked at me perplexed and said, "Who the hell are you? The courtroom is full of people and the table is full of attorneys." I didn't bother to answer. It didn't make any difference for either of us.

As they brought me into the courtroom I saw Alexa, my daughter, crying. I realized the courtroom was full, but I could not see anybody beyond her. She was fifteen at the time and in high school. Exactly when she needed me most. Emotions washed over me. Tears burst in my eyes, but that was not helping anybody! I brought my attention back to my speech. *All is good! Everything is temporary!*

Excerpt from the Sentencing Transcript, Southern District Reporters

THE DEFENDANT:

Thank you very much, Your Honor.

Over the last several months, and with God's help, Your Honor, I have taken advantage of a disastrous situation of my own making to look inside myself, and to do some soul-searching to find the real purpose of my life.

I found that I'm a totally different person now. I realized and I understood all the mistakes that I made both in my personal life and in my professional life, and I learned a lot from them. Not only that I don't recognize the person that I was, but I can't believe that I jeopardized my life and my loved ones with my prior conduct.

I cannot even think the person that I was caused so much pain and suffering. I wanted and needed to achieve more and more in life. I constantly felt that I was not good enough, that I was not worthy enough. It was like an intense craving for more, to fill a hole that I had inside.

I strived for money and success, for recognition and titles, just to feel better about myself. That is the reason why I took the title of chief financial officer of Taxi Club Management. I put a strain on my daughter and on my loved ones around me. And yet I was not happy. I was not happy with my achievements. I was not grateful for what I had, and I definitely did not enjoy anything that I did.

Most of the time I was sick, I was tired, and I was unhappy. I suffered terrible migraines, and I had insomnia for years. Sometimes

I was under heavy prescription medication just to be able to function and go to work.

At that time, if you had asked me what my best achievements were, I would have said that I came to this country with barely any money and I sometimes worked two jobs. I passed the bar, and I became an attorney. But now my best achievements are my daughter and my loved ones and my friends. I am so grateful and immensely thankful for all the help and unconditional love that they offered me, and they continue always to be there, and they continue to do it. I am grateful for waking up every morning, Your Honor.

I am grateful for the air that I breathe, for the water that I drink, for the food that I eat now. I am grateful for everything. The Roman emperor Marcus Aurelius said what a privilege it is to wake up every morning, to love, to think, and to enjoy, and I believe that is the true meaning of a purposeful and meaningful life.

Since I've been at MCC, I discovered writing. It has helped me a lot to cope with my situation. I started writing every day. I also meditated a lot and I read a lot of books, mainly philosophy and spirituality. It has made me grateful for my life because as bad as conditions are at MCC, I was able to find what I need in life to be happy, to have peace, and to have a purpose in life.

After I serve whatever sentence Your Honor feels appropriate, I'll write a book about my experience and transformation, to help and inspire others to realize that they don't have to hit rock bottom, they don't have to get sick, they don't have to lose everything like I did, or turn to drugs or any other addictions to change their lives.

I have met so many women at MCC who are otherwise good people, but they did a bad thing. I would like to become a life coach to help people realize and discover that we hold the destiny of our lives, that only we have the power to change and to find happiness and love, but sometimes we don't know how to do it.

Over the Easter holiday, my uncle Alexander Daniel, who wrote a letter to Your Honor on my behalf, died of a heart attack at sixty-two, leaving behind a ninety-five-year-old mother, his wife, and his two stepchildren. It was devastating for me, not only that I loved him, and he was part of a very few people of my family in this country, and his life was taken away too soon, but also it made me realize how precious our life is.

I know that what I have done has laid waste to time that I could spend with my daughter, my law license, and basically everything that I worked for my entire life. I am grateful to Your Honor because I had the opportunity to find how blessed the conditions of my life are, and I truly regret that my actions made me realize it through this process.

I regret that I have caused my daughter, Alexa, who is only in tenth grade, great suffering and pain. I would like to apologize to her directly for all the pressure that I put on her to excel in school and for the late hours that she had to stay with her tutor to finish her homework because I wasn't home, I was at work, and because now when she needs me most, I'm not with her. But now when I realize how precious our life is, I pledge that I will spend all my time that I have with you.

Your Honor, I know that I'm a better person now than I was before this happened, and I really count my blessings every day. I don't want to live in fear anymore—fear of death, fear of being sick, fear of not being worthy, even fear of flying. Fear is destructive to our lives and takes so many precious moments away from us.

Your Honor, I know that I'm being judged today for my actions, but I only have my words to convey my sincerity that my previous life has caused. That is all, Your Honor. I just want to thank you for all your time and attention with this case.

THE COURT: Thank you.

THE DEFENDANT: Thank you.

THE COURT:

I am not sure that I have ever heard a more articulate statement from someone awaiting sentence. I doubt it. I hope that you have truly discovered the things that you have told us about.

THE DEFENDANT: Thank you, Your Honor.

THE COURT:

And I don't think there is any real likelihood that you will ever be in front of a criminal court again.

And so, though there is, in my judgment, no need for a sentence here to prevent you from doing it again, there is a need to impose a sentence that will make others think more than twice doing anything like it."

Although the judge was impressed with my words, it didn't make any difference. The court already had the sentence written, so no efforts of my attorneys were taken into consideration. And at the end of the reading, the judge stated that the conviction is not for my punishment but to serve as an example for others.

"Queens Immigration Attorney Sentenced to Five Years in Prison for Orchestrating Asylum Fraud Scheme" proudly proclaimed the United States Attorney's Office, Southern District of New York, and the US Immigration and Customs Enforcement Agency on their respective websites. Countless similar articles inundated the internet, dominating Google search results and marking this as the headline event of the day. Well, I can't deny that I made it into the published press, even if it was for all the wrong reasons. Unfortunately, all this propaganda and charades inflicted prolonged pain and suffering upon my daughter, Alexa.

I was sentenced to sixty months! That is five years of not being in Alexa's life!

"Well, let's see the bright side of things! I am still alive, and everything is temporary! So very soon I'll be back home! Time is just a construct of the human mind."

The suggested designation to serve my time was Danbury. The judge made it very clear that the designation is just suggested and that I was now in the hands of BOP (Bureau of Prisons) to put me where they have availability. That chapter was finally over.

Three weeks later I was all packed and waiting to be transferred to Danbury, but it didn't happen. In June we heard the news that all transfers were stalled for one month. June turned into July and nothing. I kept asking the unit manager if the designation was approved for Danbury and when approximately I would be transferred, but due to security reasons they were not allowed to disclose any information.

On July 19, 2019, early Tuesday morning, I heard my name called. Exactly eight months to the day I went into MCC, I was going out. Off to where?

Chapter 17

CON TRANS

THE TRANSPORT, WHICH IS THE term the officers use for the actual transport of inmates, like the entire experience I was going through, was surreal. If you remember the 1997 movie *Con Air*, without the explosions, shootings, and the bunny, the setting was identical. Total movie-like experience.

All my belongings were placed in a garbage bag and left at intake with my ID wrapped around the top as closure. I was told those are shipped separately. I was again (the regular procedure), stripped and squatted, searched and given a blue uniform. That's all you get, regardless of the weather. No jacket or long-sleeve bodysuit is allowed. Thank God it was July.

The marshals took me to a blue transport van. Inside the van was a girl who came from Brooklyn. I asked if we were going to Danbury. The marshals said, "No, we take you to a meeting place. We don't know where you guys are going after that." *Fantastic! Wherever I go must be better than MCC.*

They locked us in the van from the outside with a big lock. The van had bars all around, but I was able to see outside. I was enjoying the sun, the trees, and the traffic. We drove north on the FDR Drive, and I recognized the Hudson Valley area. I figured it should be the way to Danbury, Connecticut. At some point I realized that we were going in circles, passing through the same intersection a couple of times. And then, we stopped. Both officers got out of the car, and I could hear them speaking. Apparently, they could not find the meeting place, wherever that was. So, we were kind of lost! Eventually we got back on the road, and I saw a sign that read Stewart International Airport. *Wait! What? Airport? Where are they taking me?*

I wanted to ask but there was a partition, a fence, and a gate, plus I was restrained, and I could not reach to knock. I tried to calm myself down and took a few deep breaths. Panicking would not help me.

All is good. I trust that I will get to a place that is best for me, I kept mumbling in my head. I didn't want to let in the creepy thoughts that were giving me chills up my spine, that put me in despair and were giving me a panic attack. That would not serve me any good!

We reached a large, fenced gate with all kinds of security signs and cameras, and then another gate and then another. Barbed wire was all around. *Geez! What is this?*

We drove by multiple military planes—massive, gray, intimidating—and lines of hundreds of men in either orange jumpsuits or regular weird clothes but chained—a lot of chains—and a lot of marshals. We stopped at the end of the line of airplanes all the way on the other side of the tarmac from where we entered, and the officers got off the van again. After a few minutes they unlocked the van from the outside. They opened the door and signaled the girl next to me to get off.

"What about me?" I asked.

"You stay here," one of the marshals replied, slamming the van door in my face.

Okay, a sigh of relief. No *Con Air* for me! And then waiting and waiting. And now what?

The officer finally came back, opened the door, and asked, "Where are you going?"

"How should I know where I am going?" Panic started to build up in my thoughts.

"Where do you have to take me? I asked.

"Here! This is the meeting place," the officer replied dryly.

"Danbury was my designation at sentencing. Maybe that is where I go?" I continued.

"Danbury! Danbury!" the officer started yelling to the other officers.

He came back, helped me out of the van with chains and all, and told me to rush because I was late and the transfer van to Danbury was at the other end of that runway.

Oh, rush, you say…with the shackles and chains in one hundred degrees Fahrenheit. A migraine was brewing.

On the right side, planes were lined up and on the left side, buses and vans were lined up. Almost all the inmates were embarked on the buses and some of them already started to leave. I was walking as fast as I could toward the end of the line. I literally reached the last van, which was the same kind of van but without that many bars and fences and partitions. One of the officers looked like Kevin Hart, the comedian. "Oh, finally, we thought you would never join us!", he said. The other officer was a woman.

The van already had four women inside who had been given a brown bag with food and were eating. They had all arrived by plane from various places. The officers were irritated because I was late. Apparently, we had to be in Danbury by 2:00 p.m. in order to have time to process us and be in for the 4:00 p.m. count. It was 1:30 p.m. The drive to Danbury was not long, but the protocol to leave the airport premises would take a while.

By the time we were on the highway a normal human conversation was on the way between us and the officers. It was something that I had not experienced in MCC. I wondered if it was a Connecticut thing or a Danbury thing. It already looked like a good place to be.

We got to intake at Danbury and were told that three of us would go to the Camp and the other two would go to the minimum, behind the fence. We were processed first. With our handcuffs, chains, and shackles removed, we went through a brief questionnaire, brief medical, and were given a green uniform and bedroll. Pretty smooth.

An officer took us outside to the double gates and said, "The Camp is on top of that hill. You can walk up either this way or that way." He pointed to the two separate roads. He turned to go back inside.

"Alone?" Victoria was quicker to speak. The other girl and I were completely perplexed. From shackles to being left alone without supervision in the middle of the street.

"Yeah, you are Campers," the officer replied and went back inside.

PART II

FCI Danbury, Connecticut, aka Cupcake Camp

You may be wondering about the significance of the iron to start this section of the book. The truth is, not all institutions have microwaves, but they typically have irons. In a pinch, people will use whatever resources are available to cook or heat up their food. With limited resources and freedom, being creative is essential. The traditional approach of using tools only for their intended purpose won't work in prison.
It's necessary to adopt a new mindset and think outside the box.

Chapter 18

OUT OF THE HELL HOLE
INTO THE LIGHT

AFTER EIGHT MONTHS OF INDOOR life at MCC, I was transferred to the Federal Correctional Institution (FCI) in Danbury, Connecticut, aka, Cupcake Camp.

The beauty of the place—the green lawns and tall trees and wooded areas—tricks you into forgetting that you're in prison.

The facility lies on a large government-owned land in the upscale town of Danbury. It is a low security federal correctional institution housing men and women in separate buildings and a women's minimum security satellite Camp nicknamed the Cupcake Camp, due to the various celebrities and high-profile inmates that were housed there throughout the years.

In addition to the main buildings, there are several auxiliary buildings such as the commissary building, the warehouse, the inmates' gym at the walking/running track, the garage, construction, electrical and plumbing building, grounds building, the officers' gym building, the officers' shooting range, the officers' training and recreation center, the staffs' village, and the inmates' visiting room building. There are vast lands in between all these structures. The institution is basically self-sustained. The inmates cook, clean, repair cars and structures, cut the grass and do landscaping for the entire property including the officers' village.

The bucolic setting brought me back to my childhood in Romania, to the communist school camps of my youth. The bare-minimum amenities, the large dormitories with approximately fifty people each, the common showers and bathroom facilities, the scarce hot water, the large cheerless cafeteria with plastic trays and folding tables, surrounded by gorgeous landscapes. As kids, we were sent to this kind of camp for the fresh air and open spaces and greenery and scenery, not luxury. Then, suddenly, I'm jolted back to the present, remembering that I fled Romania in my early twenties. I was now in the US, an attorney in my forties, imprisoned in paradise? What the actual f*ck just happened?

I began to look at it as an all-inclusive, bare-minimum retreat. I'm just here for a stay. After all, everything is temporary. Somehow, I knew it would not be five years.

I've always loved nature and the outdoors but never had time to really fully enjoy them. At Danbury, I had everything. Both the outdoors and plenty of time. Nature helped save my soul.

The endless green landscapes had a very powerful impact on my mood. From my top bunk right at the window, every day I woke up to the beauty of the sunrise through a row of tall pine trees. Magical colors filled the sky and awakened my heart every morning. Birds chirping from 4:00 a.m. provided the most gentle, peaceful alarm clock. And the eternal sunsets! The most beautiful colors from which even Botticelli and Michelangelo would get inspired.

From the level of the track, outside on the ground level, the grass has several shades of green mixed with a few patches of brown nuances. Taller grasses nearby swayed in the wind.

Explosions of color that a painter would covet on his palette would take flight as butterflies flitted from the trees to the flowers to the plants to the grass. All shapes and shades of colors. My friends here are the animals, the sky, the sun, the moon and her phases. The rain lulling me into the best sleep I ever had. The sound of the wind, rain, snow, and thunderstorms were another of nature's gifts, her ever-changing symphonies.

Outdoors, I was able to completely dissociate from the chaos indoors. The dilapidated building, the sweltering summers without air-conditioning, the drafty-to-bone-chilling winter cold without reliable heat, the dreadful food, which was crappy and/or in short supply, and the people and their drama.

I found solace in the eternal beauty of nature: the fresh air, surrounded by hundreds of shades of green and gold and brown by day, blanketed by the moon and stars at night. Prison is temporary, my inner peace is permanent. Which comes in handy in prison.

At times I witnessed the worst of human nature. Self-destructive behavior by inmates, the incompetence and indifference of some BOP employees, dreary living conditions, the absence of privacy, and lack of other human rights. But I soon discovered that I always had the choice to put my attention on the peace, the beauty, or the kindness of people. I was good at winning the prison mental game.

I would spend hours lying on the grass, watching the clouds shifting shape above. A humbling experience. Finding symbols and signs in the clouds, trying to make sense of what the universe was offering me. Kissing the earth with every step, analyzing the perfection of nature. Everything has a purpose. I wondered why people so easily get lost in the noise of their minds and veer off the path of their life's purpose. Why there is so much beauty in the world, yet the people inside the building are fighting over the TV channel.

Some people never came out of the building. They stayed inside and complained. I was told that I lived under a rock, that I had no idea what was going on around me. Hmm, yeah, maybe I didn't know who had a fight, who got sent to the SHU and for what, who was found with contraband, who cursed whom, and so on and so forth. This is only noise that keeps people down, below the winning line. With that mentality and attitude one can only lose the mental game of prison, and life in general, for all I know.

I know how many birds I saw, which colors they were flaunting today, how many different songs they sang. I know how many flowers were blooming with which scents. I followed a double-winged firefly with a black dentelle on top and brownish leopard print underneath, balancing on a tall blade of grass, holding in a crane yoga position facing east.

Prison Rule #1: "Mind your own business."

People waste an incredible amount of their time and energy every day over petty stuff. But perception is everything. We have the choice of how we perceive experiences in life and how we internalize them. Even in prison. In prison, you gain authority and respect by keeping to yourself, being quiet, not complaining, and having inspirational activities. This way you gain the people's trust, and everybody leaves you alone, both inmates and officers. Because you are different than everybody else. You are not doing what every inmate is expected to do. You are unpredictable. You rise above the mainstream. You control the mental game.

I began looking at life in prison, and in general, as a series of funny events. Why get upset when I can have a great laugh?

Chapter 19

THE ALL-INCLUSIVE RESORT

As I GOT INTO THE Camp building at Danbury, I was assigned a bunk bed and a bunkie downstairs in the dungeon. My new bunkie was also originally from Eastern Europe so we got along well from the beginning.

Then, Susan took over. Remember Susan, my bunkie and friend from MCC who was transferred to Danbury a few months before? She got word that I was coming and was there waiting for me. She took me by the hand and introduced me around. Everyone knew how difficult it is at the beginning, that you get your stuff a month after the transfer, so nearly everyone gave me something. From a toothbrush to flip-flops, to food to a nightgown, to gray T-shirts and shorts. It was the middle of July. The Danbury Camp has no A/C. Industrial fans whirred from each corner of the dorm, making more noise and stirring up dust rather than cooling the air. But what can you do? I had no control over the conditions, only over my perception and acceptance to what is.

Coming from MCC, where the A/C was blasting all the time, to Danbury in a hundred degrees, took me a few nights to accommodate and be able to sleep. This was heaven by comparison. I soon realized that the entire Camp is run by the Campers. From the welcoming committee to the Christian locker (which was in charge of donations) and chapel to the kitchen and so on. There was only one officer in the entire Camp who basically didn't want to be bothered. As long as everybody was minding their own business and there were no fights all was good.

Whatever you needed, there was a Camper who provided it or knew how to get it. From massage to pedicure, to haircut and color to alterations, cooking, personal trainer, even a doctor. Whatever you wanted, you name it, it was there. Of course, there were other things in the category of contraband that, although I knew were available, didn't seem to have been worth the risk.

But back to the all-inclusive resort. After the 4:00 p.m. count and dinner I went out for a walk in the fresh air and sun. I looked at my skin and it was transparent. The lack of natural light, sun, and air from MCC for eight months had taken a toll on my body. When medical put me on the scale I showed a whopping one hundred eight pounds.

Now I had everything I needed. The next day was the commissary day, and I got a pair of sneakers for the walk on the track and some other little things. The commissary here was different than MCC. There was more variety in products—makeup, hair color, and ice cream.

I got my stuff from MCC in three batches. Two boxes with the books, watch, and MP3 player were delivered two weeks after my arrival. The second batch with my clothing, shoes, toiletries, and some food arrived ten days later, and all the rest, which was not much, appeared more than a month after I was transferred. After I settled in, I donated a few things to the Christian locker to help other newcomers like me.

Chapter 20

My First Job

THROUGHOUT THIS JOURNEY, I HAD the pleasure of meeting fantastic people. My bunkie, Sonia (not her real name), had been at Danbury for almost four years. She was an "angry bird" with almost everybody but a sweetheart with me. She knitted in her spare time, outside on a bench under a Japanese cherry tree. She made me a pair of socks for the cold Connecticut nights in the mountains and a vest that I wore during wintertime when I was going for walks.

We didn't have jackets. The only warm clothing sold at the commissary was a gray sweatshirt and a fleece jacket. On really cold days, I would go out for a walk wearing a long-sleeved shirt, the vest, two sweatshirts, and two fleece jackets and I was fine. I had a gray wool hat and a pair of gray wool gloves. All these were sold at the commissary. When it was really cold or snowy, I wore the steel-toe work boots that I also bought from the commissary. As I write this, I am wearing the pair of socks Sonia made, thinking of her and her quirky personality.

Sonia worked in the kitchen and kept asking me to volunteer there. This way the kitchen officer, the head cook, and clerk, fellow inmates, would know me and be willing to give me a job. She kept telling me to do something, otherwise I would be assigned to Grounds. Susan was also telling me the same thing. Everybody was terrified of being assigned to Grounds.

Grounds was a department of the institution, which was run by

Campers, as was everything else. It was a lead officer who gave the general instructions of what was to be done per day. Grounds took care of the grass trim and landscape of the entire institution including the officers' village and the officers' training center. It was a massive load of work and of course it wasn't easy, especially for a woman. The Grounds building was a fairly large space that housed a garage for the lawn mowers. They had probably six-to-eight top-of-the-line large Kubotas, and another four-to-six small ones, as well as a lot of trimmers and other large equipment.

On the other side of the building were three offices and a bunch of other kinds of tools, gardening mostly. Also, tables and chairs.

A week after I got to the Camp, we had orientation. That meant we were officially ready to work and receive visits. Sure enough, all new people were assigned nowhere else but Grounds! Everybody was on fire—nobody wanted to go. Besides, it was the dead of summer. It wasn't easy to be outside in the ninety-degree scorching sun wearing a thick dark green uniform cutting the grass or pulling weeds. 7:30 a.m. was the departure time. By that time, we had to be up and dressed, beds made, room tidied up, breakfast eaten, and ready by the door.

There were two or three vans that would come and pick up Campers to take them to work. Unless you had a medical letter that you were bedridden, you had to go, otherwise you would be ticketed or disciplinary summoned. The schedule was 7:30 to 11:00 a.m. and from noon to 2:30 p.m. with a lunch break from 11:00-12:00. The crew that worked in Grounds were really passionate about landscaping and were very good at what they were doing. It was not my case, and I knew that everything was temporary. Getting frustrated with the situation would only block my opportunity to see anything else that might show up.

So, I went the first day. We all had to fill out a few forms, including a waiver that basically stated if you hurt yourself or have an accident during work, it was not their fault but yours. Another survey was about any prior experience operating lawn mowers and other gardening equipment. I truthfully advised everyone, including the lead officer, that I had never done any landscaping work and I should not be trusted with any equipment for the safety of both.

All right, then! They dropped me off in the officers' village to pull the weeds and clean up a garden of an empty home that would soon be inhabited by an incoming officer. I finished quickly and sat in the shade under a large tree for the rest of the time waiting for the truck to pick me up. Every day there was something else to do. In the meantime, I kept my options open.

As I mentioned before, the Camp is self-sustained. Sonia introduced me to the kitchen officer and took me over as a volunteer. Kitchen work was one of the better prison jobs, but in order to get in, you had to gain the respect of the workers. Although all inmates are the same, in the kitchen a hierarchy prevailed. You had to earn the trust of the more senior staff. The kitchen ran like a well-oiled machine. It had to.

Meals were planned and prepared every day, according to the national menu of the BOP. The ladies would take the produce and would play with it, using whatever ingredients and utensils they had at their disposal. It was all done under the auspices of the kitchen officer, the amazing Mr. Kennel. On any given day, a minimum of ten people were cooking and helping. One tough head cook, one clerk, four cooks who were rotating on working shifts, two salad prep, two bakers, and four dishwashers rotating on shifts.

The head cook was a super tough lady. She basically ran the kitchen. She would do the firing and hiring and cooking or supervising the cooking. She was so good at what she did that she was called in to do the catering for every event held at the officers' place.

Coming from MCC, the food at Danbury Camp seemed like a Michelin-starred restaurant. I loved the creative energy and activity, not so much the drama, which I guess one can find in any kitchen. Mr. Kennel was not one to suffer fools and their foolishness, so any drama was short-lived.

Every job at the Camp was different, but working in the kitchen came with perks that a lot of people coveted. First, extra food. Public safety codes dictated that any food remaining on the serving line be discarded by the end of the day. The main line consisted of the initial servings, seconds, and thirds. Most of the time, the food was so good that it would run out before everybody got any seconds.

Another perk of working in the kitchen was a guaranteed second, whether it was a fruit, a cookie, salad, or pizza. Sometimes there was quite a lot of leftover food, which went into the trash. Some dishes were questionable not because of the preparation, but because of the low-quality produce. However, most of the time the food was great. Despite the limited vegetables and meats available, the ladies were so talented and sophisticated that they managed to create fantastic meals out of very little. During holidays, the kitchen wizards pulled out all the stops.

Holiday meals were especially festive. In addition to the insane (for prison) spread of food, the mood was set with tablecloths, decorations, and gifts. Not exactly just like home but nice, nonetheless.

About one month into my arrival at Danbury, with a work letter signed by Mr. Kennel, I was able to be released from the work in Grounds. I started in the kitchen as a table wiper after dinner, helping Sonia clean up the chow hall and prepare for the next day's breakfast. Then I took over the beverage station, filling up the ice dispenser, water, coffee, and milk machine before meals, and cleaning it before and after meals, three days a week. This was all I was able to get because it was a hot job.

Another of the perks of working in the kitchen was the "short line." That meant that everybody working in the kitchen was allowed to come to the dining hall and eat before everybody else. This was important at dinner. You would be counted in the kitchen and get to eat while everybody else in the Camp waited for the count standing by their bunk.

Then I was promoted to server, which was the second most desired job after cook. I loved it, although I was told I was a little slow at it. When you have to serve one hundred eighty to two hundred people in the shortest period of time, speed is an important attribute to have. I was celebrating human nature, the amazing psychology of people versus food. While serving, I would analyze people's faces and reactions to the menu, and how much food they would get compared to the other ones.

I learned everybody's favorites, from what they prefer, what they dislike to the arrangement of food served on the tray (that is very important for some people) to how much food. I learned to read faces and emotions. I learned how to make people happy by offering them a smile or an extra bun or their favorite burned piece of pizza with the edge.

I also learned how to mop properly. Hilarious, right? Initially

I was made fun of and taught the hard way, being yelled at, "Hey, princess, they don't teach mopping in law school?" I am grateful that I eventually learned how to make my life easier without breaking my back. I had to mop behind the serving station every night. Did I mention that I learned the best Windex substitute is white vinegar? Of course, we didn't have any cleaning product that contained alcohol.

Chapter 21

MAIN LINE

THE NATIONAL MENU (SEE APPENDIX), that is published by the BOP and is supposed to be listed at each institution for the inmates to know what they are having. However, we didn't have it in MCC, and every meal was a mystery as to what we were going to get.

All the institutions are supplied with large cans of vegetables and fruits. Basically, everything that you see on the list as corn, beans (any kind), beets, spinach, mushrooms, carrots, green peas, collard greens, chickpeas, lentils, and fruits were canned. All the fries, Tater Tots, hamburgers, chicken, and chicken patties, all the beef, fish, and fish patties were frozen. The tuna for the tuna salad was also from a can. The bread, even the whole wheat one was Wonder Bread, so not much of a quality there. Sometimes, the kitchen ladies baked bread, maybe once a month. This only happened when the kitchen officer brought them yeast and was able to be in the kitchen and supervise the process. That is just in case somebody would subtract a little with the intention to make hooch.

In 2019 and 2020, until all the kitchen ladies were released due to COVID, we had a lady who specialized in salad dressings. Otherwise, we had the bottled ones. The baked potatoes and mashed potatoes were made from fresh potatoes. The dessert was done on the premises. The kitchen had two full-time bakers and a lead baker. Fun fact: one was a former attorney and the other a former doctor. Most of the days we had fresh fruit, and twice a week we had fresh salad with lettuce, tomatoes, cucumbers, and peppers.

There were days when food was amazing, and others when you didn't know which one was worse. For example, not a lot of people would show up for the Wednesday dinners with beef tacos and vegetarian alternative soy tacos or the chili, so serving dinner was fast.

The taco shells were often rancid, and the potato chips expired but for some people were OK with that. I don't know if there was a rule on serving bananas but bananas were delivered green. They were set in the officers' office, and they were not served until they were almost black. I have rarely served a yellow banana. That's the reason why most of the bananas ended up in oatmeal.

The most popular meal by far was the roasted chicken on Thursdays for lunch. It was a full leg, roasted to perfection. Because I was serving, I was allowed to take an extra one. Since I would rarely eat meat, I would give my share to Susan. The second most favorite was the beef stew which was my #1 favorite, especially when it was made by Mr. Kennel. Then it was the cheese lasagna, the pizza, and the chef salad. Among the least favorite dishes were the beef taco, the beef burrito, and the fish patties, aka SpongeBob, from Friday's lunch.

As for the vegetarian options, the most popular were the stuffed acorn squash, the sautéed vegetables, the garbanzo burger, cauliflower steak, and the egg and vegetable burrito. The least favorite was soy spaghetti sauce, vegetarian burger, aka, the hockey puck, fried tofu, and sometimes the black bean burger.

The dining hall lay at the end of the building, overlooking the valley and the hills. With large windows it was a pleasure to have breakfast at sunrise and dinner at sunset.

Chapter 22

THE UNIFORM

OHHHHHH, THE LOVELY UNIFORM!

The uniform color at the Camp is dark green. Each inmate receives two slacks, two long-sleeve shirts, two short-sleeve shirts, four T-shirts, and a pair of black boots. The uniform sizes range from small to extra-large and the boots from five to ten. All sizes run extremely large. The uniform may be exchanged for a new one or a different size once a year. Then for the six-month exchange we were given four pairs of white underwear and four white sports bras. Again, they were oversize, hence I had to purchase new ones from the commissary.

The shirt was part of the official uniform. During the summer the uniform was the pants and green T-shirt. However, when going to visits we had to wear the official uniform which included the shirt and the institutional steel toe boots, which were at least two sizes bigger. I wear size six, and I got a five and they were still huge and super heavy.

The first time my family came to visit, they didn't see the Camp on top of the hill, and they went to the double fence, barb wire main building, and my daughter started crying. Then they were told I was at the Camp and directed them to the right place.

When my daughter saw me for the first time at the Camp with the oversize uniform and humongous shoes that squeaked when I walked, she said, "Geez, Ma, you look like SpongeBob in his squeaky boots." We had a good laugh!

I then bought a pair of normal boots from the commissary, which were approved both for work and part of the official uniform. Later on, I figured that there were people in the Camp who were doing alterations. Although it is illegal to have government property altered, and was considered damaged and contraband, everybody was doing it and nobody had any issues with it.

When I started working in the kitchen, I was given a different uniform. Checked black-and-white pants with the green T-shirt and a white shirt on top. Again, the white shirt was only for official visits. Every Wednesday at lunch "the circus was in town" meaning that the entire management lined up in the dining hall to address the inmates' concerns. From the warden to assistant warden, captain, food manager, et al, at least ten people.

Everybody was on edge, I guess because of their fear of each other. As a result, the main line was crazy, and everybody was aggravated. The T-shirt and shirt were supposed to be tucked in as per the institutional protocol, however a lot of people, due to reasons we all understand, could not fit the shirts into their pants. Besides, no one was allowed in the dining hall in sneakers, some people could not even fit into those institutional boots. Bottom line, when "the circus was in town" it was more aggravation than resolution, simply because of nonsense.

For me, behind the serving line, it was fun to observe both sides. Sometimes you didn't know who was more frustrated and aggravated, the inmates or the administration. The assistant warden at that time was a cool guy. Wednesday's lunch was a burger with fries. Every time he showed up, we had to have one ready for him with two portions of fresh French fries.

The kitchen pants were actually very comfortable, so every day I would wear that uniform regardless of whether I was working that day or that shift. It was an approved uniform, and I was good. Monday to Friday, 7:30 a.m. to 4:00 p.m., uniforms were mandatory including boots. If you were going for a walk or to the gym, you were allowed to wear the grays even if it was during the day. After 4:00 p.m. and weekends, a uniform was not mandatory except for visits. Otherwise, it was the gray sweatpants or gray shorts and gray T-shirt and gray sweatshirt and sneakers.

Mr. Kennel's announcement for the dinner main line was: "Main line open! Main line open! No hair rollers, no slides, no flip-flops, no tank tops, no nightgowns, no containers!"

He allowed sneakers in the dining room but not slides or flip-flops. He was good with shorts but not with T-shirts cut into tank tops or nightgowns. He required us to be decent, basically out of respect for ourselves, him, and the dining hall.

Chapter 23

THE COMPUTER

USUALLY AT NIGHTTIME, ESPECIALLY NIGHTS when the dinner menu was not a favorite, people would start cooking. Whether in response to real hunger, simple boredom, or a way to self-soothe, food and snacking was always available. Because I worked in the kitchen and I always had access to fruits, and because I do not eat much, especially at night, I was not too concerned about cooking. But I would often hear my roommates talking about the line for "the computer."

The Camp's computer room had seven computers and although we were one hundred eighty women, there was rarely a line. The maximum time allowed at the computer was one hour. You couldn't do much but check the inmate messages. But because you had to pay for this time, it was considered expensive for some, and people would rarely linger on the computer.

So, then, why would there be a line for the computer?

One night, my bunkie, Sonia, decided to cook quesadillas. So, she went to get "the computer" from the next-door neighbor. She came back with a laundry bag that had something in it wrapped in a blanket.

What in the world is that?

She took out a piece of wood and a clothes iron. Oh, so that was "the computer" people were lined up for.

There were all kinds of stories on the so-called "inmate.com," the gossip line, regarding why Danbury Camp did not have a microwave. However, there was a little counter space by the hot water dispensers between the dorms where the heavy cooking took place. There you'd find a sign, a souvenir of the mythical microwave, about how to use it. The microwave itself, however, was long gone. As mentioned, the stories of why there was no microwave are numerous and came over the grapevine of the so-called "inmate.com". Each prison has its own internal so-called "inmate.com" gossip network, and I've learned to trust absolutely nothing on it. Inmates tell their version of stories and events, which constantly get reviewed and rewritten, and are more outrageous and funnier with each retelling by a different inmate. Everybody has to contribute their two cents to the story.

Chapter 24

POSITIVE THINKING AND YOGA

MY DAILY ROUTINE HERE WAS very strict, as well. Walking in the morning and afternoon for at least one hour each time, for about six miles in total, meditation during the day, preferably outside, meditation in the early morning and at night, reading, writing, dream interpreting, drinking three liters of water a day, and selective eating.

My peaceful place for meditation was a bench under a tree on the track. It was the official tree of Connecticut, the white oak located about fifty feet from the inmates' gym. Every morning I meditated on the bench and Karla (not her real name), also a former attorney, biked in the gym in front of the window facing the track and the tree. One day, after a couple of months of observing me being still for half an hour, she approached me with the request to teach her and other inmates to meditate.

I was honored, but I know that meditation is a concept that is not well received by many people. It so happened that the recreation department posted an announcement to all inmates interested in teaching a class to file a request with the officer in charge. At that point, several classes were taught by inmates from knitting to financial literacy, and art classes to Workout Boot Camp.

I was happy to share my knowledge of energies and how to maintain control of the mind regardless of what happens in life. I filed an application that included all the details of the class including meditation. It was approved for an initial class of two months that became so popular that it was extended up until the entire institution was placed in quarantine due to the pandemic. Twice a week for one hour, twenty to thirty ladies found the Positive Thinking class a breath of freedom and peace.

***

One of the attendees of my class held a weekly yoga class. Her time was up and she was being released soon. She asked me if I would be willing to take over this class. She also saw me meditating and doing some yoga and qigong. Although I was practicing for myself, I didn't know that I would be able to instruct others.

I presented the offer to the Positive Thinking class, and they were thrilled. They encouraged me to take over the class and to do it twice a week. It was a fantastic opportunity for ladies to move at least a bit. Weather permitting, I held the classes outside in the fresh air. Unfortunately, this class also was canceled along with everything else in March 2020 when the pandemic hit the entire world.

Chapter 25

VISITS

MY FAMILY AND FRIENDS VISITED me almost every weekend, and we spent all day together. Here, all day, meaning the visiting hours, from 9:00 a.m. to 3:00 p.m. We ate fake yogurt and sandwiches from the vending machines in the visiting room. Although I was allowed to eat what was sold at the vending machines, I was not allowed to touch money or even get close to the machines. My family would bring a bag full of quarters for the vending machines.

Sometimes they had really good sandwiches and real plain yogurt. At other times, actually most of the time, they had only junk food. But it didn't matter, we were spending time together! I told them about my classes and my daughter told me about her ordeal that she had to go through just because I wasn't home.

Before the visit days, we were all excited to see our families. Girls were doing their hair and makeup for hours on end, nails, ironing uniforms, polishing boots, and lining up at the window to watch our families come up the hill. After the visits were over, everybody was crying, depressed, and heartbroken at being left behind.

I personally applied my technique, performing the letting go exercise and basically flipping all the thoughts the mind produced that would bring me suffering. Crying and being heartbroken would not help me or my family, so I had to keep my mind positive and open for opportunities to appear so I could go home.

Chapter 26

My Second and Third Jobs

THE RECREATION DEPARTMENT ANNOUNCED AN open position for cleaning the inmates' gym. It was a building on track on the lower level of the Camp. The schedule was between 11:00 a.m. to noon every day of the week. I had to mop, dust, and rearrange the weights, balls, and whatever else was misplaced. I liked it because I was by myself and when I was done with the cleaning, I could do my exercises. I took the position. However, it wasn't for long.

It was mid-March 2020, when one day I was called down to the gym by the recreation officer and the rec clerk, who was also an inmate. We went over the inventory, and he made sure everything was clean and they sealed it for the duration of the pandemic. I left in August 2021, and the gym was still closed.

However, I remained employed by the recreation department until I left. I was teaching the Positive Thinking class, did the bingo party, and helped clean the rec room in the main building.

Town Driver

During the last period of my stay at the Camp, I was the town driver. It was the coolest inmate job at the facility because I was the only inmate allowed to leave the institution. My job was to drive the released inmates who had no one to pick them up to either the airport or to the train station. In a government car, with a cell phone and GPS. How cool is that?

The Hartford, Connecticut airport was about a one-and-a-half-hour driving distance. The freedom of driving on the highway and being outside in the real world with regular people was incredible. The train station in Danbury was only about a fifteen-minute drive but getting to see the town and homes, kids going to school, supermarkets, the Starbucks coffee shop, and people wearing colorful and different clothes, felt as if I was living in a virtual reality, a parallel world. It was so much fun.

I wasn't allowed to stop anywhere, not that I would have stopped. Besides, I didn't have any money to get my favorite coffee at the Starbucks I was passing by every time. They trusted me fully with this job and I wasn't going to do anything to blow off this fantastic opportunity.

But wait, don't get too excited! That didn't happen every day!

Although the job was called town driver, it wasn't very often that I would get to go out in town. Usually, I was doing errands around the yard. Driving Campers to work on the institution's property, distributing cleaning supplies, equipment, and small office furniture, even garbage among the numerous buildings of the institution.

A day of work as the town driver started at 9:00 a.m. by picking up the car from the main parking lot of the institution. Unless it was a foggy day or very heavy snow, when for security reasons we were not allowed to leave the building and we were counted every two hours, all the days were about the same. I did whatever I was asked to do, with a break for lunch between 11:00 a.m. to noon. Most of the time, in the afternoons, I was on standby in case something urgent came up. By 3:30 p.m. I would return the key in time for the 4:00 p.m. count.

Throughout my time at the Camp, I worked grounds, kitchen, library, recreation and town driver. Each job had its own fun, including the salary, which was a joke. For the full-time position, I was making about twenty-five dollars a month. Remember that inmates are "slaves of the state."

Chapter 27

ANGEL

HERE ARE MY STORIES ABOUT my friend Angel and some of her recipes created in prison. Even though I met her only during the last five months of my stay at Camp Danbury, we formed a genuine connection and I now consider her a dear friend.

One day in early March 2021, on a sunny, gorgeous spring day, I was sent down to intake, at the main building, to bring up three ladies who were coming to the Camp as transfers from the low security facility. Certain crimes or situations qualify a person for either maximum security, medium, low security, or a Camp, which is minimum security. While most white-collar crimes and short sentences are sent directly to the Camp, people initially sentenced to the low security facility can earn their way up to the Camp by serving at least half of their time with "good behavior."

One of these three ladies was Angel, an energetic, slender lady with long blond hair wearing a neatly ironed uniform. She was standing next to a lot of boxes organized by categories, with a printed inventory list taped to each one, along with her name written all over it—Cantatore. It took me one trip with the full truck just with her stuff. We immediately connected and started talking. She told me she is Italian, and her last name means singer in Italian. I told her I am Romanian and that I know what it means because of the similarities in the Roman/Latin languages. She didn't look one day older than fifty, although later on I found out she was closer to sixty. She looked like a woman who took care of herself. We spoke about food, music, the outdoors, workouts, life experiences, and spirituality—literally anything we could talk about.

She was assigned a cubicle in the same dorm as me. I could not believe how she was able to organize all her stuff into the room, but she did. She immediately took over the job of clerk of the chapel. Due to the pandemic, religious services were discontinued for a while. After months of quarantine, the services reopened with social distancing provided. The pastor came to the Camp once a week but didn't have a clerk. Angel was delighted to set up for Mass and to clean up and tidy the chapel. But she wanted to get a job that would let her leave the Camp. She had been detained in medium and low security, behind the fence, for six years. Seeing the fence from the outside would mean a lot to her.

The job of cleaning the officers' gym and the officers' center for training and education was available. The two ladies who had the job before were just sent to quarantine, preparing for release. Remember, it was 2021, and COVID was still going strong. But life within prison, as without, goes on.

I referred Angel for the job, and she was accepted. Now we were driving around the Camp listening to music and planning what to cook and when to work out. I walked on the track for about two hours every day, rain or shine. She worked out in the gym room for much longer than I did every day.

One morning I went to the CO (correctional officer) to let him know I was leaving the Camp to take Cantatore to work. It was not our regular officer but rather a regular of the low security building who knew Angel from there.

He looked at me and said, "So, you are the getaway driver?"

I wasn't sure how to respond; joking with a CO can be a delicate, dangerous dance.

"You know she robbed a bank," he continued, probably confused by my perplexed face.

"Yes, I do," I replied. "So, you are Thelma and Louise," he said.

From then on, we became known as Thelma and Louise.

Angel used to be a personal trainer, on the outside and in prison she worked out a lot. As I've said, "Prison is a mental game," so everything one does in prison in order to stay sane is to not let prison get to you. Work out, cook, read, meditate—whatever you do just to keep your mind off the nonsense of prison.

One day, she came back from the track and told me she worked out with "the Rock." Because she had subscriptions to several magazines, from *Vogue* and high-end fashion and design magazines to the last gossip newspaper in America, I assumed she got a workout magazine with Dwayne "The Rock" Johnson. She was always cracking some kind of joke.

She usually worked out in the gym, inside the Camp, early in the morning and in the afternoons. A few days later during one of my regular walks, I saw Angel working out under a tree on the side of the track. When I approached, she called me over and said, "Let me introduce you to "the Rock," and she picked up an impressively large rock that she was using as weights.

Enough with the stories. Let me give you some of her recipes.

My favorite recipe by far was Angel's Oreo peanut cluster cake. Actually, the peanut clusters were my addition to her already famous and delicious espresso cake. It was summer in Danbury Camp, which meant no A/C and no fridge, of course. I had a bag of chocolate-covered peanuts in my locker that were melting due to the heat. A delicacy like this could not go to waste.

As a side note, all the belongings of an inmate must fit into one metal locker approximately thirty-one inches by forty inches by fifteen inches in size. That means everything the inmate possesses— clothing, food, toiletries, books, you name it—must go inside or it may be confiscated. Just because an inmate cannot have too many possessions.

Well, during COVID, due to the distancing rules we each inhabited one cubicle that otherwise was meant for two people; hence we had access to two lockers. (I will explain later in the book the layout of the Camp.)

So, the peanut clusters were melting in the locker, and we decided to use them in the cake. My only contribution to the making of this incredible creation was to crush the Oreo cookies for the crust with the bottom of a cup, and to help change the ice bags for the makeshift fridge we made from a milk crate.

Angel's Recipes

"Hi, I'm Michelle Cantatore aka Angel, aka Shazam, aka Barbie. I've been inside for a while and have had time to experiment and tweak my recipes. This is one that can be done using only boiling water. My Italian pasta dish is my favorite—since I am Italian, and every Sunday was pasta day.

The Sushi bowl is really good, but you have to take your time to dice and slice the top for it to be perfect. As for my cheesecakes, I think they are good enough to sell outside!

These recipes are easy to follow, inexpensive, and can make for a great conversation when you tell those enjoying the dishes where the recipes came from.

Buon appetito!"

Espresso Peanut Cluster Cheesecake

Ingredients

For the cream:
- 5 vanilla pudding cups (19-20 oz)
- lemon juice ½ cup
- 1 plain creamer (11 oz)
- 2-4 tablespoon espresso powder (instant coffee)
- 2 packs peanut clusters

For the crust:
- 6 packs Oreo cookies (11 oz)
- butter

Instructions

For the cream:
1. Put peanut cluster bags in a large container aka ghetto cooler with boiling water.
2. Put the butter in a little bag in cooler with boiling water.
3. Empty all the pudding cups into a large bowl, stir in creamer gradually, don't pour it all in at once.
4. Beat/whip until spoon can stand.
5. The more you whip, the better it is.
6. Pour ¼ cup lemon juice into the mixture and whip some

more, add more lemon juice if needed but not more than ½ cup.

7. Pour/scoop out melted clusters in and whip some more until blended. thoroughly. Blend in 2 tbs of espresso, taste, and add more according to taste and desired strength.

For the crust:
1. Separate Oreos, scrape out cream centers, and discard. Place Oreos in a bowl and crush with a creamer container or cup or whatever object you can find.
2. Once cookies are crushed, pour in melted butter till all cookies are wet and evenly spread on the bottom of the bowl.
3. Pour batter over the crusted bowl.
4. Cover with plastic bag and ice overnight or minimum of 5 hours

Equipment required: 8- or 9-inch plastic bowl, plastic spoons, forks, whatever we could find to crush the biscuits, large garbage bags, and ice to cool. At home you can use regular kitchen containers and equipment to ease your work. Based on this the time required to make this cake varies tremendously.

Note: Please see the appendix, Sample Commissary List, to check the products and sizes we were able to buy. (Yes, buy.) If we wanted to make a special dish not served in the cafeteria, we had to use our money to purchase ingredients. Not all institutions have the same commissary list. Depending on where you are and what you have available you might need to substitute or improvise.

The lemon juice and butter were procured from the kitchen. The lemon juice was a bottled no-brand, and the butter was salty little slivers placed between two pieces of parchment paper. The word *pro-cured* does not mean stolen. It means that the butter was served out to people especially at breakfast. We would collect the butter slivers from the fellow inmates who didn't use it, or simply ask the kitchen for a few extra sleeves.

When making this recipe at home, I use natural lemon juice and unsalted butter. For a 6 pack of Oreos, I used 1 stick of butter and a little more than half a lemon.

Of course, for a healthier version, you can substitute the vanilla pudding and creamer with cream cheese.

Sushi Bowl

Ingredients

For the sushi sauce:
- 1 tsp sugar
- 2 dashes soy sauce
- 2 tbs hot pepper mix, no oil
- 2 tbs minced garlic
- 1 squeeze honey
- sweet and sour sauce to taste

For the sushi:
- 2-4 packs tuna
- 1-2 packs rice
- 1 pickle or fresh cucumber

For the middle sauce:
- 1 good squeeze mayo
- dash of chili
- dash of garlic powder
- dash of salt

Instructions

For the sushi:
1. Tuna drained and dry, 2-4 packs depending on how much sushi you want to make. Mix all with sweet and sour and garlic.
2. Cucumber or pickle diced small.
3. Prep rice in boiling water with the bag. Follow the instructions on the box of precooked rice.
4. In individual bowls put rice on the bottom, then add the well-mixed ingredients of the middle sauce, add the tuna mix, then the cucumber. Top with the well-mixed ingredients of the sushi sauce.

5. This is the most time-consuming dish, especially if you cut the pickle and the hot pepper mix with the plastic knife. At home, please use a regular knife or a chopper!

These are the original bowls from Danbury and the yellow plastic knife.

Sunday Pasta

Ingredients
- 1 pack angel hair pasta
- 6 packs marinara sauce
- olive oil
- powder garlic to taste
- minced garlic to taste
- Italian seasoning
- vegetable flakes

Instructions

Sauce:

1. Pour the packs of sauce into large cooking bags (smaller garbage bags).
2. Pour 4 tbsp olive oil, 3 tbsp garlic powder, 1 tbsp seasoning, put in boiling water. Change the boiling water every 30 min.
3. Open beef sticks, remove outer casing, cut into ½ inch pieces and put in bag in the same boiling water with pasta.
4. In a cup take 1 tbsp minced garlic and 4 tbsp veggie flakes and cover with warm water. Soak during the entire process until flakes and garlic are soft
5. After a few hours and at least about ½ hour before it is time to eat, pour beef stick, veggies, minced garlic into the sauce bag and stir. Put it back in hot water.

Pasta:

1. Break in half and put in a large bowl, cover with boiling water. Let sit 6 minutes, drain water, stir pasta, and cover again with boiling water, let sit another 6 minutes.
2. Drain all water and rinse with cold water. Drain and rinse 2 more times and drain thoroughly.
3. Fill bucket with very hot water.
4. Take pasta and put in a plastic bag, pour olive oil over, sit bag in bucket.
5. When it is time to eat, place pasta on plates, sprinkle with grated parmesan cheese (a lot) before putting the sauce on. Pour sauce on top and sprinkle with salt and more grated cheese.
6. If you cannot find grated cheese, you can grate the cheese block with the perforated top of a salt or pepper shaker.

Voilà! Enjoy!

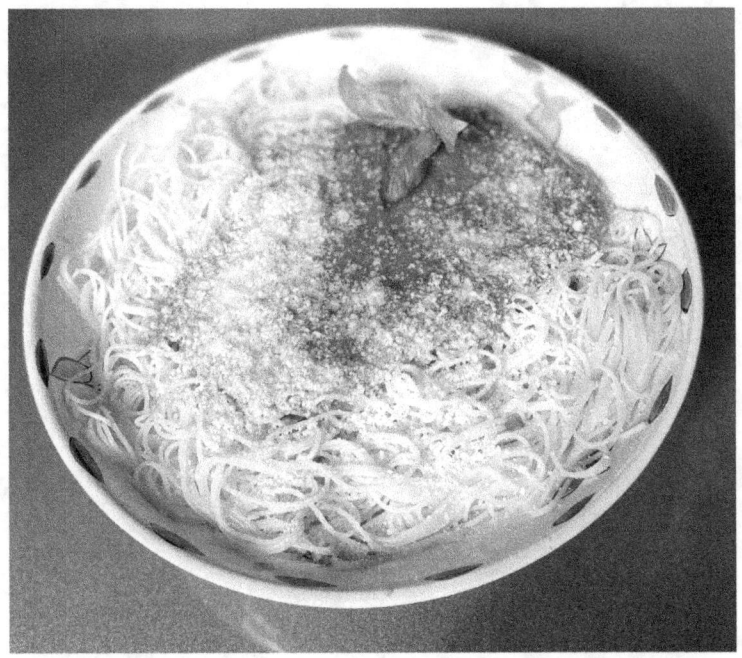

For my last night in Danbury, Angel had prepared the pasta and the cake, and we had a lovely dinner. I was on the balcony in the quarantine section, and she was in the lower hallway. We usually had farewell parties for all the girls leaving. Since COVID started I had seen more than two hundred people come and go, until I was able to qualify for my departure.

Since I have come back home, I have cooked the Sunday pasta a few times just thinking of Angel and sending her good wishes. I experimented with sushi and cake, as well.

Chapter 28

NORMA

IN PRISON, THERE ARE THREE meals served in the dining area of the kitchen. Breakfast from 6:30 a.m.-7:30 a.m., lunch at 11:00 a.m., and dinner after the 4:00 p.m. count usually around 4:30 p.m. Dinner ended at 5:30 p.m. at the latest. Except, of course, during quarantine, when the kitchen and dining hall were closed, and food was delivered to the dorms in foam containers. And that was before count around 3:30 p.m. The food was prepared either at the men's facility or mostly at the women's minimum security down the hill.

At the end of the book, I have listed a national menu sample to give readers an idea of the food served. You'll see why by 7:00 p.m. we would start getting hungry for something filling and tasty and start wondering, "What's cooking?"

Every night without fail, you would find Norma busy cooking at one of the counters, usually for a sizable crowd. Here's how post-dinner works: diners decide what they want to eat and gather the ingredients needed for the meal. Everybody shares something and the person cooking, Norma in this case, basically eats for free. That was the deal. I don't really know what arrangement Norma had made with our Camp mates, but every night there she was cooking away. So, I grabbed my notebook and followed her hands, writing down everything she was using and everything she was doing. This is firsthand knowledge, legally speaking.

I asked Norma how she knew how to make so many dishes

with so many various and sundry ingredients. She explained to me that although she was born in the US, all her relatives are Latinos, and that she has blood from practically all the South American Latino countries and Caribbean islands. She spent lots of time with her large and diverse family, and she learned their culinary secrets and ingenious methods of cooking a large meal with limited resources.

Norma, although young, showed signs that life wasn't easy. She had a medium, tough build with long black hair and natural beauty. Norma always had stories and her hands moved along with her mouth. Her stories were about her family, friends, how much she loves to cook, and how many recipes she could make outside, with normal ingredients. It took a lot of creativity and expertise to devise delicious dishes on the spot, with a crowd of hungry women eagerly waiting. Before she would start cooking, she would find a picnic table outside to write her poems and rap words. At the end of the night, I would get to taste all her recipes and they were all delicious. No wonder so many people shared in her cooking.

Norma's Recipes

"I love to cook, serve food to my family and friends, write poems, play chess, and help others. I want to open a food business when I go home."
~Norma Claudio from Lawrence, Massachusetts

Nacho Bowl
5 people

Ingredients
- 2 turkey sausage
- 1 bag rice
- 1 block provolone
- 1 pickle, regular or spicy
- jalapeño
- 1 bag olives
- 1 Velveeta pack
- ½ bag refried beans
- 1 tortilla bag
- spices: garlic, adobo, olive oil

Instructions

1. Norma said, "Here, cook rice in the ghetto cooler with hot water. Add olive oil and adobo. Leave for 10 minutes. Then take out of the bag, put in a big bowl, and mix well. Put rice back in the bag and back in hot water for another 10 min."

2. She had a red cooler like the one in the picture, of course worn-out from several years of ice and cooking, passed down or sold from inmate to inmate. Summertime with no A/C, down in the dungeon or up in the rooms with the sun beating on the metal frame, a cooler like this and a little fan were the inmate's prized possessions.

3. Turkey sausage cut in 4 long pieces and cook for at least 2-3 minutes on each side or until cooked. On a plank of wood, cover meat with wrapping paper and iron. When cooked cut into small pieces.

4. Cut provolone, pickle, jalapeño, and olives into small pieces and keep in separate bowls.

5. Velveeta block is put in a bowl, cut in small pieces. Add hot water and mix until melted. Add a little adobo. Keep it in hot water to stay liquid.

6. Put refried beans powder in a bowl that is placed in a larger bowl with hot water, to stay hot. Add garlic and hot water over the refried beans. Mix for a few minutes until cooked, not very thick.

7. It is a very messy process and requires a lot of bowls and

space, so clean along as you go.

8. Either in a large bowl or individual bowls arrange as follows:

9. Tortilla on the bottom, rice in the middle, beans on top then

10. Olives, pickle, meat, little more beans, provolone, jalapeño, Velveeta over

11. Decorate with round jalapeños on top for a kick.

Enjoy!

Spanish Rice
4 people

Ingredients
- 1 bag rice
- 1 sausage
- onion, pepper, olives
- spices: Sazón, adobo, olive oil

Instructions
1. Cut sausage in 4 and fry with the iron. Fry the vegetables a little and mix with the meat.
2. Cook rice in bag, then mix in a bowl the rice, meat, vegetables, and seasonings. Put back in the bag and rest in hot water for another 10 minutes.

Ziti

Ingredients
- 1 bag of ziti
- 1 sausage
- corn, onion, pepper
- 1 provolone block
- parmesan
- spices: garlic, adobo, mayo

Instructions
1. Cook pasta in a bowl with hot water.

2. Fry sausage and vegetables. Cut in pieces and put on top of pasta. Add provolone cut in pieces.
3. Put back in hot water. When done, serve with parmesan on top with hot/regular pickle.

Chicken Alfredo

Ingredients
- 1 bag of ziti
- 1 pack of chicken
- creamer plain (4-5 spoons)
- regular milk
- 1 provolone block
- mayo, garlic
- parmesan

Instructions
1. Cook ziti in hot water.
2. Mix the creamer with milk and make a sauce, not too watery.
3. Mix pasta with sauce and meat and season to taste.
4. Melt the provolone with hot water and incorporate it into the sauce.
5. Serve with parmesan on top.

Rice and Fish

Ingredients
- 1 bag of rice
- any fish, one type or mix
- corn, pepper, onion, cilantro
- seasonings: ½ tsp adobo, garlic, oregano, olive oil

Instructions
1. Mix fish with seasonings in a bag and place in bowl with hot water. Add vegetables.
2. Add rice and mix. Put bag back in hot water for another 10 minutes.

Note: The rice sold at the commissary is pre-cooked and conveniently portioned in special bags that can be cooked by simply adding it into hot water.

Spaghetti and Meat

Ingredients
- 1 pack of spaghetti
- meat, any
- marinara sauce
- seasonings and mayo

Instructions
1. Cook spaghetti in hot water.
2. Fry meat and cut big chunks.
3. Mix spaghetti with meat and marinara sauce, then season to taste including mayo.
4. Set in hot water for a few minutes until served.

Calzone

Ingredients
- 2 sleeves snack crackers
- 1 bag of potato chips
- milk
- 1 bag of chicken
- provolone
- spices

Instructions
1. Put the snack crackers in the potato chip bag and smash, then add milk. Mix and make a dough.
2. On a plastic bag make a circle of flat dough. Put another bag on top. Flip it on the other side and remove the plastic
3. Break the chicken into small pieces, add garlic and adobo.
4. Add chicken to the middle of the dough and pieces of provolone everywhere. Fold and close it. Replace plastic with wrapping paper.

5. Iron on one side and then flip and cook/iron on the other side.
6. If microwave is available, then cook for 4 minutes.

Mac and Cheese

Ingredients
- ziti
- any cheese, milk
- mayo, adobo, garlic

Instructions
1. Melt the cheese, add the seasonings.

Chicken Sandwich

Ingredients
- chicken from chow
- lettuce, mayo
- bread

Instructions
1. Fry and season.
2. Assemble into sandwich.

Chapter 29

GRULLON

WAKI SPOKE VERY LITTLE ENGLISH, close to none. She was originally from Puerto Rico. A heavy built woman with short hair and a very vivacious personality, she was helped to communicate by a prison friend who spoke both English and Spanish.

When the library reopened, after a few good months of quarantine lockdown, I was asked if I wanted to work as a librarian for a few hours a day. It was actually the only place in the entire Camp with A/C, except, of course, the staff's offices.

Yes! Of course, I would want to work in the library!

I sorted and reorganized the books, created new library cards, cleaned, and disinfected the place. When inmates were released at the beginning and during the pandemic, they left almost everything behind. That included a lot of books that were taken in by the education department as donations to the library. So, I had a lot of work to do. But the best part of working in the library was talking to people and observing their behavior. I heard life stories, dramas, and funny anecdotes.

Waki's friend, Vanessa (not her real name) was a very entertaining storyteller. Her hobby was crocheting. She made all kinds of animals and creatures. She brought them to the library to show them to me and borrow some of the specialty books. She loved telling me funny stories about Waki. One day she said Waki asked her when she was going to prison. "This is prison, Waki," Vanessa replied.

Like most people the notion of prison is cells with bars. But the Cupcake Camp is not like that. It's more like Girl Scouts camp—an open, common space with no bars, no locked doors. It's just that you cannot go home. Actually, you can physically leave, but that would mean adding another five years to your sentence with an escape charge.

Waki's Recipes

"I was born in Puerto Rico. I'm looking forward to going back home one day and having my own restaurant because I love to cook."
~Walkiria Grullon aka Waki

Cold Noodles Salad

Ingredients
- noodles
- mayo
- garlic powder
- salt and pepper, onion powder
- Spam or any meat you like
- chicken bouillon cube

Instructions
1. Put the noodles in cold water, when ready drain the water.
2. Then add the chicken bouillon cube to the noodles and all the other ingredients except the meat.
3. Cook meat separately if you wish, then cool off and add to the salad.

Ready to serve.

Fruit Salad

Ingredients
- apple, pear, orange, banana, peach
- original creamer ½ container
- 5 tbs sugar
- regular milk

• Jolly Rancher cherry flavor juice

Instructions

1. Cut fruit into desired size pieces.
2. In a large bowl mix the creamer with the milk and sugar. Add the juice mix (for color). Mix until cream has a thick consistency. Add the fruit, mix, and keep it in ice for 2 hours.

Chapter 30

TOES

WHEN SOMEBODY COMES TO PRISON, the so-called "inmate.com" network starts spreading the news. People want to know who you are, what brings you there, for how long, and basically as much information about you as possible. Soon the gossip and rumors, guesses and fictions are born and flourish like mushrooms after a storm. When people, especially women, are bored, their imagination tends to run wild, and the stories they can come up with are indeed ingenuous, hilarious, outrageous, and super entertaining.

When very young, petite, skinny, and funny Charlize came to prison she was annoyed by all the initial interrogation, so she came up with the story that she was in prison because she cut someone's toes off. And voilà! She became known as Toes. (This was especially funny because nobody believed her.) Toes could never ever have ended up in the Camp, with a short sentence, for doing something like toe amputation. The Camp is reserved for nonviolent crimes, short sentences, or for people who earned time and credits in higher security prisons and are transferred to the Camp at the end of serving their time.

Prison rule #2: Never believe what you hear from the so-called "inmate.com."

Toe's Recipes

"There is a funny story behind my nickname, but shortly becoming the Potato Log Queen. I like spicy meals. I have been cooking since a young age with my grandmother. I am looking forward to cooking again at home."
~Charlize aka Toes

She shortly became known as the Potato Log Queen because everybody loved her recipe.

Potato Log

Ingredients
- 1 bag of The Whole Shabang chips
- turkey sausage, tuna or salmon
- mixed peppers
- 1 pack chicken
- 1 mozzarella block
- spices: sweet and sour sauce, Sazón, garlic powder, adobo

Instructions
1. Smash chips in the bag. Add hot water, leave in bag.
2. Grate the mozzarella with the lid of adobo (the round holes).
3. Mix the chicken and spices in a bowl.
4. Roll the sweet and sour sauce bottle over the plastic bag creating a thin sheet of dough along the entire length of the bag. Cut the bag in the middle of the potato sheet.
5. Cook meat.
6. Put the meat in the middle of the sheet and cheese on top. Fold the sides over the mix.
7. Wrap the entire thing into a plastic bag. Cut in half if easier. Knot the ends.
8. Steep it in hot water. Change water 2-3 times until cooked and cheese is melted.

Note: The Whole Shabang is a brand of potato chips produced by Keffe Group's Moon Lodge only for prison commissary stores.

Now there is an entire industry created around these chips.

There are several flavors but the original one is a mix of salt and vinegar and barbecue and spices. I understand that some stores in Canada sell this kind of potato chips but in the US, they are only available online. A single bag can reach a whopping twenty dollars, if not more.

Sushi

Ingredients
- rice
- salmon/tuna/mackerel
- garlic, onion powder, Mrs. Dash, mayo, pepper, creamy paste
- sauce: hot cheese, Velveeta, sweet and sour, water, soy sauce

Instructions
1. Put rice, then meat and sauce on a plastic bag.
2. Roll.

Egg Salad

Ingredients
- hard-boiled eggs
- adobo, garlic, mayo, onion

Instructions
1. Mix together.

Chapter 31

MARIE

REMEMBER MARIE FROM MCC? IN Danbury she was always very active as well, always doing something. We were both in quarantine, each in one room on the upper floor. She knew I liked fresh fruits and every time she had one, she came to my room to give it to me. Usually, it was apples. She cooked pizza almost every day. Her equipment of choice was often the iron. One day, Marie almost got in trouble running around the Camp looking for the iron right before count.

Marie's Famous Pizza

Ingredients
- tortilla wraps
- marinara sauce
- shredded mozzarella
- whatever meat: sausage, chicken, pepperoni
- mayo

Instructions
1. Parchment paper, paper towel, or toilet paper wrapping for that matter would work just fine.
2. Iron required.
3. Spread mayo on the tortilla wrap and add all the toppings. Fold and fry / cook. Turn on the other side.

Danbury Grilled Cheese

Ingredients

- bread from main line
- butter main line
- mozzarella
- provolone
- parmesan

Instructions

1. Equipment required to grill: iron

Chapter 32

CONTRABAND, SHAKEDOWNS, 3:00 A.M. BED COUNTS

A FEW PEOPLE WERE CAUGHT using cell phones and were sent for a minimum of thirty days to the SHU. Now, the SHU we had at our institution, where I was held for nineteen days at the beginning of the pandemic because I was exposed to someone who was believed to have been infected, was shut down due to unsanitary conditions, and management was reluctant to send people to Philadelphia. That was the closest SHU for women in the area. But due to COVID, "shipments" were limited. Since I lived "under a rock," as I was told several times, I had no idea who was bringing in what and how. But it wasn't hard to notice the Air Jordans, the flashy fake lashes, the Gucci sunglasses, cigarettes, perfumes, jewelry, you name it. So many times we were strip-searched, and rooms searched, Breathalyzed in the middle of the night, and lined up in the hallway for the officers to do the search. Things were still coming in somehow!

I wasn't there to educate anybody, and I had no control over other people's actions and behaviors. I was the sage of the Camp, in terms of whoever was open and ready to ask and receive what I had to share. I had to mold myself to the environment and not let any nonsense disturb my peace. I accepted and embraced everyone as they were. We all act in life out of our own pain. Some people choose the healing path, while others unfortunately choose the destructive path.

At one of the shakedowns, they confiscated all the pillows,

allegedly because they had found some drugs or pills hidden in a pillow. I am not going to let my comfort be destroyed due to some people's nonsense. Because I suffer from migraines, and the medical department had my history of occasional Imitrex shots, I was able to get a medical certificate that required me to have a pillow due to the migraines. With this certificate in hand, I went to the officer who confiscated all the pillows and got my two small pillows back. From that point on that certificate was hanging by my bed and I never had an issue after that.

Another time, I was walking on the track where one girl was smoking. She asked me to let her know if I saw any officer coming.

I respectfully told her, "Consider I am not here. I don't see you and you don't see me."

And that was the end of someone ever asking me to cover for them.

Besides, everybody saw me meditating both outside and in my cubicle a few times every day. Although my body was there, I wasn't there.

One night around 1:00 a.m., we were woken up by the announcement to line up in the hallway with our ID in hand. An intimidating, loud, rude female lieutenant was standing by the officers' station with a Breathalyzer in her hand. We each passed by her to be tested. This woman was the terror of the Campers. She was always screaming and cursing. I personally never had an issue with her, as I didn't have an issue with anybody, inmate or officer, for that matter.

It turned out that her behavior was just an act and deep inside she was a very kind person. When we were in quarantine with COVID, she came to check on us a few times, brought us extra fruits and muffins, and tried to make our lives easier while in there.

This incident, however, triggered a massive shakedown. Apparently, the night officer was doing his rounds and found some empty bottles of booze. This was in the time when C Dorm was sealed, so to speak. It was not actually sealed, but we were not allowed to go in there. But after all, this is prison. Don't expect people to follow instructions or rules. Several times people were caught smoking in there. According to the officer who found the empty bottles, that was the hiding place of the incoming contraband.

Another night, around 3:00 a.m., we were awakened by the

light in the dorm and screams of officers to line up by the hallway for a shakedown. The assistant warden, who had just arrived on the job from a male penitentiary or a real prison for men, a big, scary, and very rude individual, was roaming the hallway like a wild animal caught in a cage. He was visibly furious! I guess if you paid close attention, you could even see fumes coming out of his ears, like a cartoon image. He looked like he was a heart attack or stroke waiting to happen. The louder he yelled, the redder he got. Geeze! What in the world would make this guy so mad? I tried to find the humor in the situation since I had no way to control what was happening.

However, being woken up at 3:00 a.m., lined up against the wall with a furious-as-red-coal guy yelling and cursing at you, without any apparent reason, bringing very inappropriate words to a bunch of women, wasn't easy to take, especially for some older ladies, weak of heart, medically speaking. Since we were instructed to stand up straight, military-style, a few of the scared and medicated ladies woken up like that in the middle of the night collapsed. The guy took it as an offense that we jumped to hold the falling ladies and got even more aggravated. We didn't have permission to move, allegedly. And whoever collapsed would be penalized for failing to follow instructions!

We all failed to follow his instructions, he claimed. I guess the guy didn't get the memo that this wasn't a violent crimes male penitentiary but a nonviolent, short sentence, mostly white-collar crimes women's prison. Besides, this was the laid-back Cupcake Camp!

He was visibly angry and complained that a package containing contraband had been dropped off at his doorstep earlier that evening. In my mind, I pictured a cartoonlike scenario with a spitting and fuming character.

He believed the package, containing Fruit Loops, flounder, and an unmarked bottle of alcohol, was intended to be delivered to an empty home across the street from his house. It was then expected to be collected by Campers who worked in the officers' village on the institution premises. His suggestion was that he had seen the vehicle with a license plate that would soon be identified. He wondered why anyone would risk their freedom for this shipment.

Apparently, he didn't know the lobster story! Keep reading!

Chapter 33

PEOPLE OBSERVATIONS

THE BEST ENTERTAINMENT FOR ME was to observe people and their behaviors. I was fascinated by observing the psychology of people.

A prison monologue from one inmate:

At the top of her lungs, someone yells, "Who the fuck you dirty bitches put the box of Cherry Coke on top of the garbage can? You don't know how to read the sign? Tear it up and put it in the garbage! You fucking bitches are nasty! This is what you do at home? Tear it up and put it in the garbage!"

Same person continues, in a lower, kinder voice, "Greatly appreciated, please and thank you."

Back to yelling, "Not on top of the garbage, not next to the garbage but in the garbage! You fucking bitches!"

In a calm, sweet tone, "God bless you, thank you very much."

Even more aggravated and louder, "Again, for future reference, you nasty motherfucking bitches...put the boxes in the garbage."

The monologue ended when a corrections officer who was passing by from atop the stairs yelled, "Shut up."

How can't you be amused by this type of behavior?

Another humorous moment I observed one morning happened on my way to the bathroom. A woman was standing in front of the laundry basket, trying on the clean mop heads as hats. It was a reminder that being open-minded allows us to notice and appreciate the small moments in life, rather than being consumed by pointless thoughts. This was better than stand-up comedy! One can rarely make up these kinds of things.

Officer Bargsten, aka Mr. B

I couldn't not write about Danbury Camp without mentioning Mr. B. He was held in high esteem by the Campers, as both defender and disciplinarian. He was renowned for his fairness, and his main purpose in life seemed to be ensuring the proper functioning and safety of the Camp. Even if he caught someone with contraband and had to send them away for thirty days, they would not be angry with him.

Mr. B found ways to get to know inmates better, understanding everyone's individual situation and who was likely to break rules or cause trouble. He read emails and listened carefully to conversations, so he could determine where "things" were brewing or problems arising, applying justice evenly and without bias. Some people adored him while others loathed him, but all agreed that he kept Camp standards high. Once he told me my conversations weren't exciting enough—they were more like reading *The New York Times*!

His 9:00 p.m. count speech was a legend. Everybody knew it by heart. This is how it goes:

"All right, ladies. This is that time again. Time for the 9:00 p.m. stand-up count. Drop what you are doing and stand up for count! Count tiiiime, Count tiiiiime!"

This was around 9:00 p.m. whenever the second officer would show up. They would count upstairs; the rooms first and then would go downstairs to the dorms…

"A Dorm! Count! B Dorm! Count! C Dorm! Count!"

The protocol of each count was that two officers would pass by the dorms and count the inmates. The 4:00 p.m. and 9:00 p.m. during the week and the 10:00 a.m. during the weekend were stand-up counts. The night counts, midnight, 3:00 a.m., and 5:00 a.m. were not even announced since people were sleeping. The officers would just pass by with the flashlight to make sure everybody was in their bed.

When the count was over both officers would go back to the correction office and announce the count to the center. Sometimes there was a recount and we had to stand up in front of each bunk.

Most of the time it was correct.

"All right, ladies, clear count! As always one chair per person in the TV room, no gatherings or conversations in the hallway. If you have more than three people in your cubicle you have to take your conversation elsewhere. As always, dress appropriately, and keep it classy! Lights out on the base!"

That is when the lights in the dorms were turned off and everybody was going their way, either to the TV, recreation rooms, shower, phone, or sleep. I was personally going to the computer room to send the good-night messages to my family, refill my water bottle for the night and morning, and then go to sleep. Depending on when the second officer would show up for the count, I would usually go to bed around 9:30 p.m.

Chapter 34

THE PANDEMIC AT CAMP

THE PANIC SLOWLY SETTLED IN over the Camp with all the confusion and some unbelievable news on this virus. The world was predicting a pandemic! What??

We heard from families, friends, and the TV that the world was slowly closing. Visits were canceled the same week the NYC public schools closed, but otherwise it was business as usual at the Camp.

The kitchen was still open. We served food wearing hair nets as masks. Everybody was eating in the dining room, classes, and programs were open. It was a time of total chaos because we didn't know what the reality actually was. It wasn't until the beginning of April 2020 that we got the first disposable masks and were told that was good for two weeks. Yes, you understood right, one mask per person, good for two weeks.

Around the same time, we heard on TV about the CARES Act and the list of qualifications for inmate release into home confinement. But nothing happened, until one day people's names were loudly called over the speaker. All the inmates with less than eighteen months left to serve were going to quarantine for a minimum of two weeks pending release into home confinement.

In mid-April, the entire Camp was placed under quarantine. Fifty people were cramped into one big room 24/7 with only a few minutes for a phone call and computer. The food was delivered to the dorm, as well as commissary purchases, which were limited to strictly necessary items for twenty-five dollars a week. We had people on the other side of the partition on three sides. We received one more disposable mask for another two weeks and then were given cloth masks that we washed and hung to air-dry. There was no sanitizer, and the cleaning products were limited.

From my top bunk with a window and view of the valley, where I watched the sun rise every morning, breathed the fresh air, and listened to the birds, I was now in a top bunk in the dungeon, in the middle of the dorm, with no natural light, and with hot pipes ten inches above me.

It turns out that the people who were medically at risk if infected were the people with longer than eighteen months' time left on their sentences, and they were not allowed to leave. Because of that, the inmates sued the institution. A few attorneys and law professors at Quinnipiac and Yale Law Schools were working on this case pro bono. It was the first lawsuit of its kind, and it was successful.

In one month, at least half of the Camp was gone. When I got to Danbury in July 2019, there were closer to one hundred eighty people. In January and February of 2020, at least another twenty people came, so the Camp was almost at full capacity, which at that time, was two hundred people.

By August 2020, the new inmates coming in were immediately processed to be released to home confinement under the CARES Act. The requirements were to have less than eighteen months or have served more than 50 percent of the sentence, have a certain medical condition listed by the CDC that made you medically vulnerable and high risk if infected with the virus, and have a nonviolent crime.

Approximately 70 percent of people coming in qualified for this rule. Whoever did not qualify under the CARES Act was included in the lawsuit and released that way.

During my stay at Danbury, I saw more than two hundred people leave. By the fall of 2020, there were less than forty people left in the Camp.

You would ask, of course, but what about you? Why didn't you leave?

Well, great question! I wasn't medically vulnerable. I didn't have any medical condition, and I had more than 50 percent yet to serve, so I didn't fit in any category.

One day at the end of May 2020, we were all lined up in the hallway. It was time for the first COVID testing. We heard that down the hill, at the male and female buildings, most of the people were sick, but at the Camp we had no case yet.

By now, the dorm I was in was almost empty, with only three people left, and one of them was waiting for approval to leave.

I had moved to one of the cubicles by the window and I was alone. The rules loosened a little bit. We were allowed to go outside to get fresh air and walk. Actually, except for the counts I was outside all the time.

Chapter 35

THE CAMP LAYOUT
AND DISTANCING

THE MAIN BUILDING OF THE Camp is located on top of the hill overlooking the hills, the forest, and the town of Danbury. The building is long and flat-structured on three levels. The highlight of the Camp is the outdoors—the track, the view over the hills, the forest, the upscale town of Danbury, and nature in general. Birds chirping, fresh air, flowers and trees scents, and all kinds of visiting animals from the usual deer, skunks, and raccoons to foxes, bobcats, and even a bear. It's a mountain camp setting with the most beautiful sunrises, sunsets, and night sky.

On the lower-level ground floor of the building or "the dungeon," there are three large dorms of twenty-five cubicles each—A Dorm, B Dorm, and C Dorm. A cubicle includes a bunk bed, two lockers, and two plastic chairs. Each cubicle houses two people, so each dorm is meant to house fifty people. However, during the pandemic, with the social distancing practices implemented, each person occupied one cubicle. The Camp building was designed as a communal space, hence social distancing practices were kind of impossible to follow.

The dorms have huge open spaces. The cubicles are separated by some dividers not much taller than the upper bunk. Everything on top is open space. It has neither A/C nor any kind of air flow, except windows on only one side of the building. Two industrial fans placed on each side of each dorm were on all the time, regardless of season or temperature. The fans were circulating the same air of the open space including dust, viruses, and whatnot. We tried to keep the few windows on the side open to get in fresh air, but many people with the bunk by the window would not allow the window to be opened.

In the wintertime, the heat was uneven, that is when it was on. And when they turned it on, it could not be turned off. So basically, *on* in November and *off* in April. Whatever happened in between, "tough luck!" I remember one October being really cold.

A Dorm, where the heat line started, was scorching and C Dorm, which was at the end of the line, was freezing. Two bathrooms were designed to be between the dorms. However, only one bathroom was functional, because the one between A and B Dorms was closed down due to disrepair, mold, and other sanitary issues. Hence, the entire population of the Camp was left with one bathroom with six stalls, six sinks, and three showers. The hot water in the showers was also an issue. Most of the time there was no hot water and sometimes it was unbearably hot. So, you go figure as to the distancing rules.

The mezzanine level has a long hallway with management offices, a gym room that was transformed from a dorm, without any equipment just the padding, computer room, library, laundry, TV/entertainment room, Skype room for video calls, classrooms, and the stairs to the kitchen.

There is an entrance at one end of the hallway through the education side of the building. This is the newer portion of the building and had some sort of A/C. That entrance/exit is used to get to the parking lot of the Camp, to the commissary building, and to access the outside recreation area with picnic tables spread all over.

On the other side of the outside area is the staple red railing to the stairs down to the track and gym. The outside gym building is fully equipped, from treadmills, bikes, and ellipticals to weights and exercise DVDs and books, with a designated TV and DVD player. At the beginning of the pandemic the outside gym was closed down. Formerly known as D Dorm it was padded and renamed *gym*, although it remained empty.

Returning to the hallway, the education side has one bathroom that had only three stalls and three sinks. It also had three showers but due to the fact that the bathroom was at the end of the pipeline, no hot water or water pressure would reach this particular restroom.

However, it was my personal favorite because it was the only bathroom with A/C and automatic water faucets. In COVID times, washing hands and not touching anything was fantastic, and most important it was the only bathroom with porcelain stalls and toilet seats. All the rest were prison toilets, meaning metal and no seat. This was called the education bathroom.

Next to the bathroom is a room split in two—the computer room and the law library. The computer room is a small space with nine computers, a printer, and a corner with a typewriter without a ribbon. The ribbon is for sale at the commissary. One of the computers was exclusive for legal research of cases. During the pandemic, of the eight computers, four were closed, so only four computers were available for use.

In the prison system, access to the computer means access only to your inmate email. That is done by logging in with a combination of ID, password, and PIN. The time limit for each log-in is one hour, however most of us used it for only a few minutes. The time online and the printing is paid with Trulincs, which is the currency of the correctional system. Each inmate has an account where family and friends can deposit money—it is also called "the books." It is also the account for the direct deposit of the money the inmate makes for the work done, since it cannot be called a salary.

The other half of the room is the law library that was initially meant for computer classes, law books, and a resources center for the research and filing of forms. It had at least one full-time worker who was an inmate with some sort of legal, financial, or office background. During the pandemic this room was open only as access to the copier. To operate the copier, you needed to buy a copy card from the commissary.

Next to the computer room is the office of the education department officer.

On the right side of the education hallway are two classrooms and the office of the recreation department officer.

Continuing down the hallway on the right side is the recreation room, a spacious room with four TVs, tables, and chairs. One wall is covered by arts and crafts supplies lockers assigned to inmates who either teach or take art classes such as painting, cardmaking, knitting, or crocheting. A large closet houses board games, playing cards, yoga mats, and other various recreation tools.

On the wall next to the recreation door is a schedule panel where all the announcements of the Camp were posted. From the TV schedules to class schedules to other news. Several management offices, the library, laundry, and Skype room are aligned on the same hallway.

On the upper level there are six rooms of three bunk beds each and medical offices. On the other side of the upper level are the phones, the Camp manager's office, phones, and another large entertainment room with TVs, bathroom, ice machine, chapel, and prayer room.

Between the dorms on the lower level are counters for cooking, a sink for washing dishes, an ironing board, and a storage closet for cleaning supplies.

At the end of the hallway is an exit to the backyard, picnic area, track, and gym as well as the steps to the kitchen and dining room or the chow hall.

Chapter 36

SURVIVING SOLITARY CONFINEMENT

ON JUNE 3, 2020, AROUND 6:00 p.m., we were getting ready to cele-brate Susan's departure the next day when Christi, one of the three ladies left in my dorm, was called down to intake. We all thought that she was approved to be released and we were happy for her. A few minutes later, a couple of officers stormed into the dorm asking who else was housed in that dorm. It was me and an older lady who was waiting for her compassionate relief approval to leave. We were told we had ten minutes to pick up essentials and go down to intake. We weren't told anything else, no reason whatsoever. We took a few things and, as instructed, went down to intake. There we were locked in one of the cells. Again, nothing, no information as to why we were there.

After 9:00 p.m. count they brought two cots and we were given two ripped and dirty blankets. We asked for a lieutenant, which is someone with a little more authority. Nobody came. We were locked in a cell that was in the back of intake and had no toilet. If we wanted to use the toilet, we had to yell for the officer in the front to unlock the cell. He showed up only at counts—midnight, 3:00 a.m., and 5:00 a.m.

Early in the morning our medical officer showed up and told us that Christi tested positive for COVID and although we tested neg-ative because we had been in the same dorm with her, they had to place us in quarantine, as precaution. He assured us that we would not remain there but made sure to advise us that the procedure by

CDC states a minimum of fourteen days quarantine is required.

Nobody showed up again for the rest of the day. We had to yell at the officer up front to let us use the toilet and give us water.

After about twenty-four hours of this nightmare, we were transferred to the SHU. The cells on the first tier, however, were used for quarantine. We were both shoved into one cell that had a bunk bed, a toilet, and a minuscule sink. We were locked up 24/7 with access to a shower only three times a week, where we were taken in handcuffs by two officers, and locked again in the shower cell for a maximum of ten minutes.

The entire unit shared one regular pay phone mounted on a metal frame with wheels connected to the wall with a thin long phone wire that was passed through the bars of the cell by the duty officer. The upper cells where the disciplinary inmates were housed for months at a time were allowed to use the phone only once a month.

The lower tier, the quarantine, didn't have restrictions as to the use of the phone. Still, the five hundred minutes per month applied. However, we were given five hundred free minutes a month during the pandemic as part of the CARES Act. Before that, we had only three hundred minutes that we had to pay for.

My cellmate was able to call home and her daughter reached their attorney. By the next morning she was out. Her judge was outraged about the treatment we received and ordered her release immediately.

So, I was alone in the cell for a total of nineteen days, although I tested negative twice. It was there, in solitary confinement, that I perfected my strategy on *How to Win the Mental Game of Life* and A.P.P.L.E., *5 Pillars for Success*, which is now my teaching method and an on-line course.

I had no control over anything but my mind. I could not control all the nonsense, lack of privacy, the unknown that could happen at any moment, the horrible food, only hot water from a tap that I had to cool off so I could drink and wash, all the profanities and fights through the cell walls from the other inmates, all the things that were outside of my control, and all the feelings and emotions that came up. I had a choice to let them take over me or not.

I can't even begin to describe how terrible the food was. To give you an idea of its horrid quality, let me recount a typical meal, served in transparent plastic containers: wilted, sometimes molded lettuce and nothing else, accompanied by two soggy slices of white Wonder Bread that I'd promptly discard without opening. My sustenance mainly consisted of boiled eggs, which we were fortunate enough to receive twice a week, along with some fruits, a sort of cake, and milk.

Our cells were enclosed by bars, and an electric door, also constructed from bars, served as the entrance. I considered myself lucky with my cellmates on both sides. Jen, to my left, would pass me her minuscule carton of milk that we received every morning as part of breakfast, as well as her boiled eggs because she had allergies. Sandra, on my right, would share her apples and sweets since she was diabetic and couldn't consume them.

Officially, it was against the rules to exchange items between cells but sometimes even the officers would do us the favor of passing food to me from other inmates. Oh, and just for your information, my cell number was thirteen. In the midst of this bleak situation, you'd often hear people yelling, "Who wants an apple?" or "Who wants my milk?" I would echo back, "I do, at thirteen!"

Yes, I would be angry and frustrated at the incompetence, the lying, or carelessness but I would not buy into it, not feed it with energy, not keep it alive because it doesn't serve me, or anybody, any good. Letting go is the act of returning to my peace. I might not be happy, but I was at peace. After all, everything is temporary.

Since half of my time in prison was during the pandemic, I practiced this exercise for hours on end. With all the restrictions, fear, bad food, cranky people, and all kinds of challenges at every step, it was my opportunity to work on myself and strengthen my mind. Here is my letting go exercise.

Imagine a container with holes, reminiscent of the energy we possess. When filled with water, it flows through the holes without any hindrance. When soil is added, the water still flows, but now the holes also allow for seedlings to sprout, nurturing life. However, if the holes are blocked, the water mixed with soil would turn sour, much like the bitterness and resentments we hold inside.

It's crucial to let go and allow things to move freely, even if it's just for a few moments of peace. Is the exchange of a lifetime of rotten mud for a few moments of peace worth it? The decision is yours.

Chapter 37

THE LIBRARY AND THE KITCHEN

WHEN I RETURNED TO THE Camp after nineteen days in solitary, the Camp was a ghost town. Only thirty people were left, when not long ago there were close to two hundred. I was told that upon our departure, the C Dorm had been sealed and that all of our stuff had been disposed of because of the fear of infection. I wasn't concerned much about my clothing and food but about my books and notebooks with my writing. I was assigned another cubicle by the window in A Dorm. Because so many people were released, and left their stuff behind, I was able to get clothing. And then to my relief, one of the officers from the day I left told me that he had saved my books, and they were stored in one of the locked classrooms sealed in cardboard boxes. I was happy for the books. It didn't matter that I had to buy the food that I had lost.

It was June 22, 2020, and the Camp was reopening. A few people were going to work, and we heard news about the reopening of the kitchen. The food in solitary was horrible and now, back at the Camp, I had different options.

I was offered the position of librarian. On Monday, June 29, 2020, I started working in the library. It was the only place in the Camp with A/C, so it had a welcoming atmosphere.

It was a lot of work, which took me a few weeks to organize, but it was worth it. Cleaning, sorting, rearranging, donating the doubles, and creating new library cards. But the best time was talking to people, hearing their stories and life experiences.

The food continued to be delivered from the kitchen down the hill at the women's minimum, but I was asked to help serve it. The kitchen reopened in October with bells and whistles. A couple of new ladies offered to cook for the entire Camp. By this time, we were about sixty people. It was very interesting that nobody in Camp got sick. We were eating the food that came from the other institution that had several cases of COVID and all the officers from there were passing by the Camp. Oh, and Christi who suffered incredible conditions for fourteen days in a suicide watch cell, might have been a false positive. She was released shortly upon returning to the Camp.

Occasionally the medical officers were sent to take our temperature, otherwise back to normal. New classes that offered credits started. I took all the programs, not because I needed the credits but because it was interesting information such as trauma, assertiveness, parenting, brain functions, Spanish, US law, and real estate law. I restarted teaching the Positive Thinking class. The yoga class, however, was not approved because of the yoga mats. Actually, no exercise or physical education classes were allowed.

Chapter 38

A Thanksgiving Feast and Christmas 2020

We had an amazing Thanksgiving experience in 2020. There were about sixty women at the Camp, and everyone was given the opportunity to contribute toward the celebration if they wished to. We had a variety of turkey dishes, as well as sides such as bacon-studded and vegetarian greens, baked and mashed potatoes, salads, and a range of mouthwatering desserts. There were eight types of pies, cakes, cookies, and ice cream. My friend Amy and I had the privilege of serving the sweets.

The joy and happiness were evident not only in the delicious food but also in the smiles on people's faces. It was a scene straight out of a movie! The kitchen officer, Mr. T worked tirelessly to ensure that our holiday celebration went smoothly, despite the inevitable kitchen drama that always occurs, I am sure, in every kitchen with more than one cook. I am incredibly grateful to Mr. T and the ladies who pulled off an exceptional Thanksgiving feast.

In December, Mr. T came up with a plan to bring a Christmas tree into the kitchen. He managed to sneak in a tree and some decorations from the officers' training center, which was not in use due to the pandemic. As the town driver, I continued to assist with serving dinner. I always found it interesting to observe people's behavior, especially when it came to food.

As every day something new happened, the fun didn't last long. One evening in early December, I had dinner with Amy and four other women at a table meant for six. We shared food and snacks from our respective rooms. While munching on an apple, Amy mentioned that it lacked any flavor, which I found odd considering that the one I had the previous night was sweet and juicy. However, little did we know that on December 7, the entire Camp would be put under quarantine due to COVID, following four positive cases. On December 11, to safeguard us, we were given KN95 masks that were purported to last for sixty days. Nevertheless, on January 14, just over thirty days later, we received new masks.

Unfortunately, a few days later, fifteen individuals, including Amy and all the ladies at our table, tested positive for COVID, with most losing their sense of taste and smell. In contrast, the rest of us tested negative and could return to work. The positive cases were promptly removed from the Camp. During this period, I would often drive out of the facility as several people got released. I felt genuinely happy for them, while also anticipating my turn to leave. Every day, I would test my senses by sniffing vinegar.

Just in time for Christmas, Amy and several other women arrived back at the Camp on December 23. Some individuals were released right away, while others completed the processing procedures soon after their arrival.

Chapter 39

TESTING POSITIVE

THE TEST RESULTS CAME BACK, and unfortunately on December 28, 2020, I was one of those with a positive COVID result. Despite not having any symptoms, I still had to follow protocol. Along with thirteen others, I was brought to intake and put into quarantine until January 5. It was quite the greeting with handcuffs and chains just to pass security in the men's visiting room! But cots and blankets were provided for us, which gave me some peace of mind while spending New Year's in isolation. *My technique of being at peace, regardless of whatever happens in life, will surely help me through it!*

I was thankful that despite testing positive, I wasn't ill and still felt great. The irony of the situation was unbelievable; there were only toilets in the visiting room, yet a mobile shower was installed within two planks of wood, connected to both the water supply and draining system. And believe it or not, the phone had been placed there as well! It was hanging on a plank of wood nailed to the mobile shower. That was the most hilarious part! All at once practical, funny, and surreal; it's no surprise I felt grateful for how things turned out.

The next morning, we moved to a new location, with handcuffs and chains again. The only thing I could do was trust that everything would work out in the end!

We were moved across the street to the visiting room of the women's facility. It was freezing cold because it was all windows and heat was scarce, but boy, what a beautiful view! The night before we were transferred, I dreamed of a tree. As I sat against the trunk of a majestic tree, I felt secure, safe, and grounded. As soon as I walked into this room, I noticed a book called *The Secret Life of Trees*, which had a tree on the cover that resembled the one in my dream.

I positioned my cot toward the window, reveling in the breathtaking view of the lawn and farm that was adorned with Christmas lights. Each morning, I was privileged to witness a splendid parade of deer and wild turkeys passing by, and sunrises, majestic moonrises, and sunsets. We also had a snowstorm that was out of a fairy-tale movie set. The tree on the right side was the highlight of my view, as it resembled the one in my dream and on the cover of the book I found.

The tree provided me with a sense of security, tranquility, and confidence that everything would work out fine. To validate this feeling, a shamanic friend sent me a message through my family, whom I was speaking to every day, informing me that he had visualized me under a tree, feeling at ease. How much more confirmation do I want?

It didn't matter that I was in prison, that I had COVID, that I was locked up in a sort of solitary quarantine, and that I had no idea when I was going home. I was at peace! I knew everything would be fine. Nothing else mattered!

Having worked in the kitchen for so long at the Camp, I was able to pick and choose what to eat. I registered as a vegetarian because the meat was not of the highest quality. However here, they served me vegetarian meals, and I didn't have a choice of what to eat. Every day was rice and beans for lunch and dinner, which I don't eat. Sometimes I would get string beans or a baked potato but those were rare. Otherwise, I would count on my breakfast, oatmeal, muffins, milk, and fruits.

The women at that facility knew we were housed in their visiting room and for New Year's Eve, they made us decorations. They had an officer deliver them. It was awesome!

Everybody who followed a regular diet got a juicy steak at New Year's. I was a vegetarian, so I got double portions of rice and beans! Fantastic! I was grateful for the banana muffin saved from breakfast and an apple, so I was fine. *It's all temporary,* I reminded myself. On January 5, 2021, we were back at the Camp safe and sound.

Chapter 40

SNOW SHOVELING

THE WINTER AND SPRING OF 2021 were especially harsh. Snow fell almost every day. There were piles and piles of snow. In late April there were still patches of ice and snow left on the ground, that's how cold and how much snow we got. Now that quarantine was over, guess who had to shovel and plow the vast premises of the institution? The Campers!

In normal winters, those who had access to the equipment in grounds, garage, or construction would do the work. They made an announcement on the radio for volunteers when the snow was as insane as it was, since it was way too much for the few people to handle. What kind of person would like to shovel in a blizzard? Result? No one volunteered!

The snow was expected to keep falling relentlessly for the next twenty-four to forty-eight hours. Additionally, it was announced that names would be randomly selected every three hours, day and night. "If you volunteer now, you won't be called during the night," they said. Regardless of your job tomorrow, your name could be chosen.

On snowy days like these, we were not allowed to go outside, including to work. My friend Amy and I volunteered to shovel to avoid any middle-of-the-night calls. We were assigned to clear the front entrance and stairs of the women's building across from the Camp. Despite the blizzard, we marched on with shovels in one hand and a bucket of deicer in the other.

By the time we finished the stairs, the upper part by the door would already be covered in snow. Upon returning to Camp, I noticed Amy's mascara had smudged all over her face due to the snow blowing all over. It was a funny sight, and we both had a good laugh when we saw ourselves in the mirror. We didn't have much makeup, and the commissary was selling products that are usually found in ninety-nine cent stores in NY. But we had no options. So here, it was either no makeup at all, or the little bit of bad quality makeup we had. I was grateful for what I had.

The 3:00 a.m. shift was the toughest one. The mere thought of leaving my warm and cozy bed to shovel was unimaginable. The announcement alone was enough to jolt me awake.

Chapter 41

VALENTINE'S DAY SALMON PATTIES

THE PRISON EXPERIENCE BRINGS TOGETHER people from all walks of life. I was fortunate enough to have met ladies that I never would have met otherwise— interior designers, attorneys, doctors, teachers, accountants, art dealers, and other interesting people. It was the Divine design for us to meet. We formed a bond, an unspoken closeness, a family. Extreme experiences like these bring people together, makes some human, others humble. From my experience, suffering brings out the best in people.

Food brings comfort. Like a celebration, it provides a short-term break from harsh realities. It enhances the little pleasures of life. Cooking and eating together builds a bond between people. Sharing this very basic need helps to strengthen and solidify friendships.

With very little, women in prison become extraordinarily resourceful. On Valentine's Day 2021, having survived COVID in solitary, we were all back in the Camp and ready to party. Amy, Randy, Barbara (not their real names), and I, four middle-aged women found guilty of white-collar crimes who happened to meet and connect in Danbury, became quite close. In this very awkward place and situation, we decided to make the holiday and our time together, however limited, a fun experience.

We scheduled our turn to use the iron. Valentine's Day was an especially busy time for the iron. Many people were finding ways to celebrate through improvised cooking, and we had to schedule time.

We started cooking on top of the lockers in Amy's cubicle because it was the only one that happened to have an outlet.

As I mentioned before, due to COVID distancing mandates, each person was designated one cubicle that was normally meant for two people. Each cubicle had a metal bunk bed, two metal lockers, and two plastic chairs. We were able to fit one more chair and all four of us enjoyed a wonderful Valentine's Day dinner consisting of salmon patties and some snacks.

Because the iron was small and old, we could not fry more than two patties at a time, and they needed twenty minutes on each side. We cooked for hours, telling stories, and laughing. We took care of each other—to be safe, to eat, to have everything that we need under the circumstances.

After we finally finished eating a few hours later, we went to the organized Valentine's Day party with bingo and playing cards in the big recreation room upstairs. Because I clerked for the recreation department, I was in charge of the bingo equipment and calling the numbers. People had snacks and nonalcoholic drinks. Some people were watching TV on the other side of the room. It was the atmosphere of Girl Scouts campfire night, without the fire. We did the best we could under the circumstances.

Salmon Patties

Now, all four of us have been released from Danbury. For a while, we were still under BOP supervision and were not allowed to communicate with each other for at least two years. I personally hold those souls dear in my heart. In honor of our time doing time together, I decided to make salmon patties at home, prison-style.

Of course, the iron is just for show but otherwise the recipe is intact.

Ingredients
For 4 people
• 3 pouches pink salmon
• 2 rolls Ritz crackers
• onion powder
• garlic powder

- mayo
- salt and pepper
- lemon juice

Instructions

1. Drain the salmon and crush the crackers. Mix all ingredients together in a large bowl. Spices vary by taste.
2. Work in batches to make the patties.
3. Equipment required: a piece of wood, an iron, parchment paper, paper towels or toilet paper wrapping.
4. For at home prep, a frying pan over heat and a spatula.
5. Fry on each side for 20 minutes. Time varies based on the iron or method of frying.

Chapter 42

THE LOBSTER

PRISON RULE #3: SEE SOMETHING, *say nothing.*

There had to be a separate chapter for this story. One day during the pandemic, when things were running normally in the Camp, all of a sudden, we were back in lockdown. No work, no outside recreation, no commissary, no computers, no phones, no videos. What in the world could have happened again? I thought.

The attorneys handling the legal case had informed us that an inspection of the Camp would be forthcoming to check the living conditions there. As I previously mentioned, a class action case was opened against Danbury Institution and its warden. It was organized by some of the inmates with support from lawyers and professors of law, due to the impossibility of practicing social distancing in such a confined space and the terrible state of disrepair making it dangerous and unhealthy. Lo and behold, that very day the inspection occurred. An independent company had been appointed by court order to examine everything on-site, necessitating government representatives accompanying them, since it was federal property.

Management was careful to make sure they stayed strictly within their mandate—captain, assistant warden, and several lieutenants being part of this group. Pictures were not allowed on federal property by visitors, so the captain was assigned this role instead.

They were passing through the bathrooms when they reached the one that was least used due to its unsanitary conditions. A strong unpleasant odor filled the air as they walked in, which was the combination of sewer and fishy odors. As the captain took pictures, the rest looked around when one of the stalls started bubbling and burst. Everyone was surprised by what was discovered!

There were lobster shells! That's right. Someone had lobster and flushed the evidence. The captain and assistant warden were thrown to the wolves for not monitoring the Campers properly and by not checking the premises before the arrival of the investigating guests. I don't know if it was this incident, the lawsuit, a combo, or something else, but the entire management of the institution transferred out shortly thereafter and new people were appointed.

The lobster in the Camp was never attributed to anyone but surely the story remains and will remain in the book of the Camp.

Chapter 43

BEING TRANSPARENT

AT FIRST, IT WAS ALMOST impossible for me to distract myself from my own inner demons and the chaos surrounding me. Privacy, solace, or harmony were impossible to find while living under constant supervision. Not long before that, I had been a successful attorney and an executive with an admirable salary and reputation. Now, however, I was nothing but an inmate—stripped of my personality and importance—incarcerated in a place of despair, humiliation, failure, wrath, and hostility where everyone seemed scared, hostile, ambitious, or dubious.

At the end of the day, it did not matter where I was, what I had gone through, or who was around me. What mattered was that I had a choice to let all these feelings wash over me or wash them away. In the midst of a "hurricane," I was often asked how I was so calm and peaceful all the time. That's right, indeed.

As impossible as it sounds, I simply changed my perception from, "Oh my God, what have I done? My life is over! I'm so angry! Get me the hell out of here," to "It is what it is now. What can I do to improve my life from now on? Nothing is worth disrupting my peace, at this point."

In order to achieve positive, peaceful outcomes, I approached challenging situations with acceptance, compassion, nonjudgment, and a lot of humor. At times, I was quite happy in prison.

You may be wondering, "Happy? You've lost your mind! How

can anyone be happy in prison?" Let me explain.

To begin with, let's distinguish between pleasure and happiness. We often confuse the two. As humans, we feel pleasure physically, in our bodies, through our senses, through our visual, auditory, kinesthetic, olfactory, and gustatory perceptions. A good meal, a visit to a museum, a stroll in the park, an ego rush after a compliment or a big win, a fun concert, or hot sex are just a few examples. It doesn't matter how delicious, beautiful, sensual, escapist, etcetera, pleasure is always short-lived. It usually disappears once the source of the pleasure, the physical stimulation, is gone.

In contrast, we experience happiness on a much deeper level. Not just through our senses and our bodies, but through our souls, where we live in peace, compassion, empathy, and generosity.

It is true that happiness is much deeper than superficial, purely physical pleasure, and it lasts a long time. In contrast to the physical, it is always accessible; there is nothing to purchase, consume, or possess. It is there all the time. It is true joy, and it is not triggered by external stimuli. It is just a choice.

It's a common misconception that indulging in physical pleasures will lead to long-lasting happiness. Things like devouring an ice cream cone, buying a new car, getting high, winning the lottery, or gaining power over someone else may provide temporary satisfaction, but their effects will eventually wear off. Instead, we aim to live peacefully and joyfully, prioritizing our own well-being and inner sense of calm.

Over time, this will reduce our reliance on external sources of pleasure, which can ultimately lead to pain and addiction. Research has also shown that the more we seek physical gratification, the less impact it has on us, perpetuating a cycle of consumption. By cultivating joy and contentment within us, we can improve our mood, overall health, and energy levels, allowing us to create more and consume less. Ultimately, it's up to us to choose how we perceive and experience life.

As a result, I developed the quality of being "transparent." Transparency, in this situation, is the ability to let things pass through, the ability to not let anything or anybody annoy me.

Sometimes, we might feel the need to protect ourselves by building walls of defense. However, if we choose to be open and honest, the energy released won't have the power to affect us. Rather, it will just fade away. Our reactions toward others are often influenced by our values, past experiences, and habits. It's possible to take things personally when we interpret someone else's words based on our own history. Tensions can escalate, and our defenses can collide with the pressure created, leading to outbursts of anger.

An example of this happened in my dorm at the FCI Danbury Camp during the pandemic. Typically, each cubicle was for two people, but due to social distancing measures, twenty-five inmates were living in this space, close enough to share elbows! One night around 1:30 a.m., a group of six recently transferred ladies gathered into one cubicle and began talking loudly and listening to music. I noticed that no one else was saying anything, so it was up to me to take action if I wanted the situation to change. Complaining to an officer was not a choice.

I would calmly and politely ask them to lower their volume. If I couldn't do anything about it, at least I could say I tried; there would be no reason for me to feel aggravated. I walked to the noisy cubicle, and all I was able to say was, "Please, if you don't mind," when I was greeted with f-bombs, insults, curses, names, and my personal favorite, "If you can't take the shit, don't come to prison." I turned and went back to my cubicle. After a few minutes, however, the gathering dispersed, and the noise subsided. I fell asleep soundly.

The following morning, I nearly forgot about the prior night's events when one of the ladies from the loud group approached me with an apology. As an opportunity to welcome her into our dorm, I gave her a briefing of our rules—encouraging quiet and keeping our individual spaces tidy—that we all adhered to for everyone's benefit. Later in the day, many members of my dorm were thanking me for taking action, as they had been too fearful to do so themselves.

There are many, many stories like this one, where letting the energy flow through me and being transparent helped me in my strength to not get aggravated and help the people around me dissipate their energy. It is very easy for a situation like this to spiral out of control if both parties have a rough energy level.

I did not allow myself to be infected by the environment. You, too, have the power to create, transcend, and find peace.

Chapter 44

THE APPEAL

THE APPEAL TO JUDGMENT WAS duly filed. It argued the multiplicity of charges and the application of the last charge, the identity theft. An appeal to a federal court decision is heard by a panel of three appellate judges. By the time the case got its turn, the pandemic was in full force. The hearing kept being delayed. One of the three appointed judges passed away and finally on March 22, 2021 I got an email from my attorney that the appeal was denied and judgment affirmed.

After all that happened, was I still expecting our criminal legal system in this country to be fair?

That is not only my question but also that of the Court of Appeals judge, see below:

Excerpt from the United State Court of Appeals for the Second Circuit Decision, Case 19-1486.

"JON O. NEWMAN, Circuit Judge, concurring:

Prosecutors have extremely broad power to decide which criminal statutes to charge a defendant with violating. That awesome power is only slightly limited. The prosecutor must have probable cause to believe that the defendant has violated the statutes selected and should have a good faith belief that sufficient evidence of each statutory violation exists to permit a jury to find guilt beyond reasonable doubt.

Beyond these limitations, however, every prosecutor is properly expected to use judgment in deciding whether to charge all the statutory violations that conceivable could be charged.

The pending appeal strikes me as an example of a prosecutor's decision to charge multiple counts that approaches, if not exceeds, the limit of fairness.

However, because the prosecutor's selection of statutory violations to be charged in this case encounters no legal obstacle that the court is entitled to invoke, I concur in the Court's opinion and judgment, but write separately to express views on the questionable fairness on the multiple counts in this case...

My first concern focuses on the inclusion of Count 2, charging a violation of 18 U.S.C. § 1001, in addition to Count 1, charging a violation of 18 U.S.C. $ 1546(a). Congress enacted section 1546(a) to punish those who, like the Appellant, falsified documents concerning immigration laws, in this case, applications for asylum. This statute precisely applies to the conduct of the Appellant, who prepared and submitted a large number of false asylum applications. Congress enacted section 1001 to punish those who "make [] any materially false...statement" "in any matter within the jurisdiction of the executive, legislative, or judicial branch of the Government of the United States." This statute broadly applies to the conduct of the Appellant in preparing and submitting the false asylum applications. The question is: Was it fair to charge a violation of section 1001 in addition to charging a violation of section 1546(a)? *

Six months after filing the indictment containing Counts 1 and 2, the Government filed a new indictment adding Count 3, captioned "Aggravated Identity Theft," which charged that the Appellant "did transfer, possess, and use, without lawful authority, a means of identification of another person, during and in relation to a felony...to wit, DUMITRU used and transferred the names, dates of birth, alien registration numbers and government passport numbers of applicants for asylum during and in relation to the asylum fraud and false statement violations charged in Counts 1 and 2 of this Indictment" in violation of 18 U.S.C. § 1028A(a)(1).

Having charged the Appellant with preparing false asylum applications in Count 2, the Government charged in Count 3 that the Appellant had used and transferred the asylum applicants' identifying information in preparing the same applications. And, with one possible exception, all of these applicants wanted the Appellant to file asylum applications on their behalf.

(The first indictment was filed on March 27, 2018; the superseding indictment was filed on Sept. 13, 2018)

Why did the Government add Count 3? The answer is not difficult to discover. Although Counts 1 and 2 each subjected the Appellant to a maximum prison term of five years, Count 3 subjected her to a mandatory consecutive prison term of two years. 18 U.S.C. b 1028A(a)(1).

The Government wanted those additional two years of punishment. As it turned out, Judge Kaplan's aggregate sentence of five years could have been achieved by imposing concurrent five-year sentences on Counts 1 and 2 in the absence of Count 3. He reached the same result by imposing concurrent three-year sentences on Counts 1 and 2 and the mandatory consecutive two-year sentence on Count 3.

Now that the Government has obtained the aggregate five-year sentence on this first offender who has not committed a crime of violence, it finds itself obliged to prepare a thirty-seven-page brief resisting the Appellant's claim on appeal that the facts of her case do not establish a violation of the statute titled "aggravated identity theft."

Clearly, the Appellant did not steal anyone's identity, nor did she try to pass herself off as some other person seeking a benefit. No government official thought that the Appellant was using a client's name to obtain asylum for herself.

What Dumitru did was file false asylum applications, the precise conduct made unlawful by the statute alleged to have been violated in Count 1.

For that unlawful conduct, the Government charged her with violating three different statutes. The three-count indictment was lawful.

The question remains: Was it fair?"

Chapter 45

GOING HOME STRATEGY

WHEN AND WHERE IS BEING overweight a good thing? Well, the CARES Act provided, of course with some restrictions, that being overweight was a get-out-of-jail-free card. As I mentioned, I have seen more than two hundred people leave. I didn't have any medical condition. Clearly, I was not a candidate to be included under the lawsuit.

One day, they posted the requirements again for release to home confinement under the CARES Act which were: having less than eighteen months left to serve or having served more than 50 percent of the sentence, having a certain medical condition listed by the CDC that makes you medically vulnerable and high risk if infected with the virus, having a nonviolent crime, having no disciplinary actions, and proof of full vaccination.

January 5, 2020, the day I came back to the Camp from quarantine after having COVID, was the day I had served 50 percent of my sentence. All the other requirements except the medical risk I already had. I asked my family to send me the CDC list of considered medical vulnerabilities. I remembered that I smoked back when I was in high school and early college. Although I didn't have any proof and was more than twenty years ago, I filed a request anyway. Well, no surprise! Denied!

Then, I remembered I had a cancer scare in 2013. I sent a request for medical records and when I finally got them, I filed another request. Guess what? Denied as well since it was not a current medical issue.

Almost every week, somebody from the staff looked at me puzzled as to why was I still there!

I made an appointment to see the unit manager. She was now managing both the Camp and the female low security down the hill, and she was rarely at the Camp. As I walked into her office, she said, "Dumitru, what do we do with you?"

Initially I didn't understand what she meant but then she continued to ask me if I had any medical condition. I confirmed that I didn't, otherwise I would have been out by now.

She replied, "I don't know, gain some weight!"

Hmm…gain some weight. I still didn't know if she was joking or not, but she had planted a seed of opportunity in my head.

I sought advice from medical regarding my BMI ratio. According to the CDC, a BMI of 25 percent indicates the beginning of being overweight, which increases the risk of serious illness or death if contracting COVID. I was surprised to discover that my BMI was already at 23.4 percent. Due to the restrictions and lack of physical activity, combined with poor quality food, I had gained weight without realizing it, as my oversize clothes concealed it. While trying to figure out how to gain weight faster, it was suggested I try a combination of salt, sugar, and water to achieve my goal quickly, rather than relying solely on muscle gain. With Alexa's birthday approaching on July 25, I only needed to gain fifteen pounds by then, so it was time to devise a plan.

Game on! Picked from the commissary, the opposite of my regular shopping, was soda, the Asian soups loaded with sodium and Honey Buns…lots of them.

You would think that with at least two to three sodas a day, one 2500 sodium content soup, two Honey Buns, and lots of water, it shouldn't be that hard to gain weight.

It took my body a couple of weeks to get used to the new way of life, but eventually I got it right! I was visiting the medical office to weigh myself every week and by mid-May I reached 26.1 BMI. Everybody was happy and processed the papers that were approved and signed. I was given June 10 as the tentative day to leave. I was looking forward to Alexa's high school graduation on June 24.

Little did I know that the entire process was not that easy, especially since I was leaving under the CARES Act and not the lawsuit. The case kept coming back for additional information. Every time it took seven signatures to leave the institution again. Although everybody knew me and was happy to see me go, they had several procedures to follow.

Everybody leaving had to do fourteen days of quarantine. I was placed in quarantine in preparation for departure on June 1. Early the next morning they called me into the office to let me know that again, the papers had been rejected and corrected and left yet again to do the seven signatures round.

On June 7, I was advised that my file needed to be relocated from the SDNY (Southern District of NY) where I was tried, to the EDNY (Eastern District of NY) where I belong with my residence.) I was able to get my sentencing attorney involved and the actual relocation of the file was approved within three days. On June 11, the file again made the rounds for the seven signatures. I guess by now they were sick of signing my file. Why is she still here?

Alexa kept asking me if I would be home for her graduation. Not knowing what tomorrow brings was not easy. I knew I was going home just not when.

I applied for a furlough that was denied because I wasn't leaving under the lawsuit, plus I didn't have approval or a date from the RRM (Residential Reentry Management). This is the halfway house that would process my home confinement and the ones who would be monitoring me.

Finally, on July 6, RRM got the file. Nobody knew how long it would take for them to give me a date. On July 7, they confirmed that processing takes at least thirty-five days. The Camp secretary called me into her office on the morning of July 15 to let me know that I had a date to be in the Bronx, at the halfway house. It was August 5, by 11:00 a.m.

After three months in quarantine, my initial plan came to life a week later.

I am grateful for what was and for the bulletproof patience I had built!

Chapter 46

NEXT STEP: HOME

IMMEDIATELY AFTER 8:00 A.M. ON August 5, 2021, I was called down to intake. This was my day to leave. Among the items I took with me were five boxes of books and notebooks with my writings, two little stuffed animals that a lady made for Alexa, and the socks and vest that Sonia made for me in 2019. At intake I signed some papers and received a bank card with my account balance and my mug shot printed on it. This place never ceases to amaze and humor me. Despite going out the same gate several times, I was free this time!

I embraced and kissed Alexa, not wanting to part. March 8, 2020, marked the last time we had hugged, nearly eighteen months before. I wanted to simply allow the present moment and not to anticipate how things would play out; Alexa and my partner, Sorin, my parents, and close friends Victoria and Christian have all experienced pain throughout this journey, which is their story to tell. I am thankful for their trust, support, and unconditional love they bestowed upon me and apologize that they had to go through this ordeal with me.

I got to RRM on time, I had to go through an entire procedure, but I knew I would go home, so it didn't matter how long it took. In addition, I knew that I would be wearing an ankle monitor. I'd heard horror stories about that monitor, but again, it didn't matter. I was going home! I didn't put too much thought into that device.

When I reached the office of the gentleman who would monitor me, two other people were there from an outside company testing new monitoring devices, which were cell phones. Hmm…that sounded interesting! I was one of the first ones to receive these devices. I was trained in how to use it and how to report.

I was out of there by 3:00 p.m., on my way home! What? Home? I left home to go to court the morning of November 19, 2018, and haven't returned since.

I have a vivid memory of arriving in the United States on August 5, 1998. And here I was on the twenty-third anniversary of that day—I felt as though I was embarking on a fresh start. A new life, a new beginning! It was truly a heartwarming sensation!

EPILOGUE

IT TOOK ME QUITE A while to fully grasp the fact that I was finally back home. The simple act of walking in regular shoes and wearing everyday clothes felt strangely different. I had to reacclimate myself to the routine of crossing streets, the flow of passing cars, and the presence of people in the streets. It felt like I was encased in a bubble, rolling along without any control. The world I once knew had morphed into an unfamiliar landscape with odd behaviors and skyrocketing prices.

I hadn't been home for nearly three years, and this disorientation was my reality. It made me ponder the experiences of those who had been away for fifteen or twenty years. How bewildering must the transition back into society be for them?

My thoughts then turned to Ms. Clara, though I can't exactly say I met her. While I heard her voice and her stories during our time in quarantine, our paths never crossed visually. She was preparing to go home in the SHU when I was there for nineteen days. Ms. Clara had endured a staggering twenty-five-year sentence, behind bars at the medium-to-low security. That span of time had seen technological advancements like cell phones and pagers. She mentioned that when she entered prison in the mid-1990s, cell phones were a luxury she had never experienced.

Speaking of cell phones, it also took me a considerable amount of time to readjust to technology and the use of an iPhone. It might sound amusing, but before my incarceration, I was a faithful Black-

Berry user. I had never learned to text on a touch screen, and although my second phone was an iPhone, I only used it for internet browsing and taking pictures. My primary business and personal phone had been my beloved BlackBerry, which, as it turns out, no longer exists.

During my home confinement, I was granted permission for shopping, doctor's visits, and even a one-hour walk, but the schedule had to be planned and approved ten days in advance. I had to report regularly on the device they provided, responding to prompts at random times throughout the day and night. Occasionally, I was also summoned for a drug test at the Residential Reentry Management (RRM) office, which meant peeing in a cup with a female officer next to me. However, I wasn't allowed to drive during this period. My home confinement was supposed to last until February 23, 2023, followed by a year of probation.

Then, in mid-January 2022, the manager of my case called me and asked if I was sitting down. She informed me that the Bureau of Prisons had finished calculating and applying the Good Conduct Time Credit under the First Step Act of 2018. She said, "You are credited one full year, so you'll be done next month, on February 23, 2022." This unexpected and wonderful surprise marked the beginning of the next chapter in my life.

***

It's time for my writing, observations, and inspiration to come to life. So, I took out my notebooks and started writing. This is the first book of a series of books that I have already started in prison, worked on since I have gone home, or started as an idea during my work.

As I mentioned in my sentencing speech, I feel my purpose is to help and inspire people. I reinvented myself, got educated and accredited and I am now a life coach, with emphasis on attorneys. As a lawyer coach, I bring a breath of fresh air and peace to the stressed professionals. As I very well know what the life of an attorney is, I am actively engaged in helping and inspiring them to live life with confidence, clarity, and control.

I also brought to life my strategy of survival and transformation. The A.P.P.L.E. system is now offered both as an online course and as one-on-one coaching. I am happy to help save people from themselves.

For coaching, programs, articles and more information please visit my website: www.andreeaparc.com.

ACKNOWLEDGEMENTS

I acknowledge all the officers and staff who fed and kept us safe.
We are all part of the system regardless of which side
of the fence we are on.

Special Thanks

This book would not have been possible without the following
people's generosity, kindness, support, and trust in me:
Gabriela Parcalaboiu
Alexa Dumitru
Cheryl Benton
Sorin Ghisoiu
Christian and Victoria Gheorghias
Theresa Quadrozzi

ABOUT THE AUTHOR

Andreea Parc is a remarkable individual who wears many hats, drawing upon her extensive experience and knowledge to support and motivate professionals, especially attorneys, who find themselves overwhelmed by the stress and burden of heavy caseloads. Her mission is to help them reclaim control, confidence, and clarity in their lives.

Today, Andreea stands as a powerful and grounded figure, her sights firmly set on the future while applying the lessons of her past. However, her journey hasn't always been as straightforward.

Andreea's story began in Bucharest, Romania, where she was born and raised. At the age of twenty-two, fresh out of law school, she embarked on a new chapter across the ocean in the United States.

She diligently worked her way up in New York and eventually became a successful attorney and executive in the elite business world. Yet despite her numerous achievements, success ceased to bring her joy or fulfillment.

Inside, Andreea felt a growing emptiness, constant stress, and unending misery. Her health suffered, and she found herself making irrational decisions driven by pain and frustration. Life began to unravel.

Her world seemed to crumble as she faced investigation, eventually leading to conviction, disbarment, and three years in prison—resulting in the loss of everything she had built.

However, within the confines of a windowless cell, perched on a top bunk with an open toilet nearby, Andreea experienced an unexpected transformation. She discovered a profound sense of freedom and peace that had eluded her throughout her life.

In that moment, she realized that this wasn't the end but a new beginning. With newfound peace and clarity, Andreea made conscious choices to transform her life. She learned that people change only when the dissatisfaction with their current situation surpasses their resistance to change.

No longer trapped and out of control, Andreea gained a fresh perspective and developed a unique system she named A.P.P.L.E.-5 Pillars for Success. She shares and provides individuals with the precise tools and strategies that she used to transform her life, all without the need for therapy, numbing medications, or sacrificing everything they hold dear.

Please visit www.andreeaparc.com

APPENDIX

National Menu

Commissary List

Recipes from the MCC Kitchen

My Recipes

NATIONAL MENU LIST 2019
Sample

Federal Bureau of Prisons - National Menu Lunch and Dinner FY 2019

Week 1

Sunday Lunch	Monday Lunch	Tuesday Lunch	Wednesday Lunch	Thursday Lunch	Friday Lunch	Saturday Lunch
♥Scrambled Eggs or	♥Beef Tacos or	Chicken Patty Sandwich or	♥Hamburger or	♥Baked Chicken or	Breaded Fish Sandwich or	♥Scrambled Eggs or
#Peanut Butter	#Soy Tacos	#Chicken No Flesh Patty	#Beef No Flesh Patty	#Pinto Beans	♥Baked Fish or	#Peanut Butter
♥Oven Brown Potatoes	♥Black Beans	♥Steamed Rice	French Fries or	♥Baked Sweet Potato	#Baked Beans	Turkey Bacon (2)
Cream Gravy	♥Whole Kernel Corn	♥Pinto Beans	♥Baked Potato	♥Green Beans	♥Macaroni Salad	♥Baked Tater Tots
Biscuits (2) or	♥Taco Shells (2)	♥Lettuce/Tomato	♥Sliced Onions	♥Whole Wheat Bread	♥Carrots	♥Flour Tortilla (1)
♥Whole Wheat Bread	♥Shredded Lettuce	Salad Dressing	♥Catsup & Mustard	♥Margarine Pat	♥WW Hamburger Bun	♥Salsa
and ♥Jelly (2)	Shredded Cheese	♥WW Hamburger Bun	Pickles	Dessert or	Tartar Sauce	♥Fruit
♥Margarine Pat	♥Salsa	Dessert or	♥WW Hamburger Bun	♥Fruit	♥Fruit	♥Beverage
♥Fruit	♥Fruit	♥Fruit	♥Fruit	♥Beverage	♥Beverage	
♥Beverage	♥Beverage	♥Beverage	♥Beverage			

Sunday Dinner	Monday Dinner	Tuesday Dinner	Wednesday Dinner	Thursday Dinner	Friday Dinner	Saturday Dinner
♥Roast Beef or	♥Vegetable Soup	♥Meatloaf or	♥Pasta w/	♥Black Bean Soup	♥Chicken Fried Rice or	♥Vegetable Soup
#Black Eyed Peas	♥Chicken Wrap or	#Black Beans	♥Meat Sauce or	♥Beef Taco Salad or	#Tofu Fried Rice	♥Tuna Salad or
♥Steamed Rice	#Three Bean Salad	♥Mashed Potatoes	#Soy Spaghetti Sauce	#Soy Taco Salad	♥Green Peas	#Hummus
♥Green Beans	♥Green Peas	Tomato Gravy	♥Spinach	Shredded Cheese	♥Whole Wheat Bread	Potato Chips or
Brown Gravy	♥Italian Pasta Salad	♥Whole Kernel Corn	♥Garden Salad	♥Salsa	♥Beverage	♥Baked Potato
♥Whole Wheat Bread	♥Beverage	♥Whole Wheat Bread	♥Ital Dressing Low Cal	♥Whole Wheat Bread		♥Lettuce Leaf
♥Beverage		♥Margarine Pat	Garlic Bread or	♥Beverage		♥Whole Wheat Bread
		♥Beverage	♥Whole Wheat Bread			♥Beverage
			♥Beverage			

# Indicates No Flesh Entree Item, ♥ Indicates Heart Healthy.

SAMPLE COMMISSARY LIST

F.C.I DANBURY COMMISSARY LIST: APRIL 2019
PRICES ARE SUBJECT TO CHANGE WITHOUT NOTICE! ALL SALES ARE FINAL, NO RETURNS.

LAST/FIRST NAME: _____   Register #: _____   Unit: _____   Shopping: AM PM (YOU MUST CHOOSE ONE)

Stamps: __ .55 Cent (Single)	__ $11.00 (One Book)	__ $0.01	MAX LIMIT $11.00

PHOTO TICKETS (Max 10): ____ ($1.00 each)   COPY CARD (Max 2): ____ ($6.50)

FRAGRANCE OIL (limit 2 each)
___ Fragrance/Oils	4.25
___ Prayer oil	3.25
Write in selection _____	

BRIEFS MALE (limit 1 each)
(Med-2XL)	SZ_____	8.00
(3X&UP)	SZ_____	10.00

OUTERWEAR & SOCKS (limit 1 each)
___ Acrylic Scarf	7.80
___ Winter Hat	7.50
___ Wool Gloves	4.95
___ Polar Fleece (Med-XL)	22.10
___ Polar Fleece (2XL-3XL)	26.00
___ Polar Fleece (4XL-6XL)	32.50
___ Crew Socks	1.95(S)
___ Ankle Socks	1.95(S)
___ Long Socks	4.55(S)
___ Poncho	4.95
___ Thermal top size____	9.60
___ Thermal bottom size____	9.60

TANK TOPS (limit 1 each)
MD-4XL size_____	11.05-15.45

SHORT SLEEVE T-SHIRT (limit 1 each)
SM-6XL size_____	2.95-4.50

SHORTS (limit 1 each)
SM-3XL size____	10.40
4XL-6XL size____	15.60

MESH SHORTS (limit 1 each)
LRG-2X size____	15.60-16.90
4XL-5XL size____	17.95-18.95

SWEATS (limit 1 each)
(PANTS) SM-4X size____	19.50
(SHIRT) SM-4X size____	16.80

MISC. ATHLETIC GEAR (limit 1 each)
Pro Harbinger	17.45
Circle Size: MED LRG XL 2X	
___ Fitted Hat SM/MD or LG/XL	10.35
___ Athletic Supporter	6.00
CIRCLE SIZE: MED, LG, XL	

MISC. (limit 1 each)
___ Grey Gym Bag	10.95
___ Grey Laundry Bag	11.70
___ Clear Shave Bag	6.00
___ Towel	11.70
___ Shower Poof Sponge	.90
___ Washcloth	2.60
___ Plastic Hanger	0.30
___ Flatware 4-piece	1.25
___ Mug	2.95
___ Water Bottle	3.90
___ Ajax Dish Detergent	1.64
___ Soap Dish	0.70
___ Dish Sponges 4pk	1.95

SHOES & BOOTS
Mark Shoe Style then write size below:
___ Under Armor	58.00
___ Nike Flex Trainer	67.95
___ Nike FlyBy Basketball	68.90
___ Wolverine Boots	69.95
SHOE/BOOT SIZE _____	
___ Shoe Laces (White)	1.40
V Strap Shower Shoe (Circle Size)	
X-large 7.50	

SHAMPOO (limit 2 each)
___ VO5	1.85
___ Suave	2.15
___ Head & Shoulder	7.75

CONDITIONER (limit 2 each)
___ VO5	1.85
___ Suave	2.15

DENTAL (limit 2 each)
___ Unwaxed Dental Floss	1.60
___ G.U.M.'s Dental Picks	2.65
___ G.U.M'S Soft Picks	3.30
___ Colgate Toothpaste	2.70
___ Cool Wave Toothpaste	1.65
___ Colgate Sensitive	4.90
___ Toothbrush (Med) or (Soft)	0.95
___ Mouthwash	1.50
___ Colgate Mouth Wash	5.05
___ Fixodent	4.70
___ Denture Cream	5.60
___ Denture Cup	1.95
___ Denture Brush	2.05
___ Toothbrush Holder	0.50

SOAP (limit 3 each)
___ Dove Soap (Single)	1.85
___ Pure Antibacterial (3pk)	1.75
___ Pure Coco-Butter (3pk)	1.75
___ Irish Spring Soap (3pk)	3.65
___ Next 1 Anti-Bacterial Soap	1.00
___ Next 1 Moisturizing Soap	1.00
___ Next 1 Coco Butter Soap	1.00
___ VoS Body Wash 3-in-1	1.45
___ Irish Spring B/W	5.65

SHAVE (limit 2 each)
___ Men Bic Razor (10pk)	1.85
___ Gillette Mach 3 Refill	17.25
___ M5 Razor (Handle)	8.70
___ M5 Razor Refill	8.70
___ Men Protect Shave Cream	1.95
___ Men After Shave	2.85
___ Men Shave Gel	1.75
___ Magic Shave Powder	3.35

LOTION (limit 2 each)
___ Coco Butter Stick	2.50
___ Tone Coco Butter Lotion	2.90
___ Jergens Coconut Lotion	4.90
___ St. Ives Collagen Lotion	7.10
___ St. Ives Collagen Face	5.20
___ Olay Quench Lotion	4.75
___ Ambi Face Cream	5.90
___ Curel Eczema Lotion	7.50
___ St. Ives Collagen Face	6.20
___ Coco Butter Tub	5.15

SKIN CARE (limit 2 each)
___ Biore Pore Strips	6.45
___ Noxzema Face Wash	1.80
___ Petroleum Jelly	1.65
___ Baby Powder	1.90
___ Men's Bump Stopper	4.05
___ Hot Six Oil	6.85
___ Hand Sanitizer	1.60

DEODORANTS (limit 4 each)
___ Secret Deodorant	2.00
___ Suave Deodorant	2.00
___ Degree Deodorant Men	3.60
___ Speed Stick Deodorants	3.10
___ Power Up Deodorant	2.90

HAIR CARE (limit 2 each)
___ Black Gel	2.40
___ Pink Oil	5.50
___ Sulfur 8	6.10
___ Hair Food	2.70
___ Mango Lock Twist	7.15
___ Blue Magic Hair Grease	2.10
___ Murray Pomade	2.60
___ Styling Gel	3.25
___ Dr. Miracle Breakage	7.85
___ Dr. Miracle Gro	8.45
___ African Pride	6.90

GROOMING AIDS (limit 1 each)
___ Brush/Comb Combo	2.45
___ Mirror	2.45
___ Toenail Clipper	1.10
___ Tweezers	1.15
___ Nose Scissors	6.70
___ Pumice Stone	1.90
___ Cotton Q-Tips	1.80
___ Afro Pick	0.50
___ Shower Cap	1.50
___ Emery Boards	0.90
___ Rubber Bands	0.75
___ Pony Tail Holder	3.20
___ Wave Cap	3.25
___ Cotton Balls	1.50

OTC MEDICINES (LIMIT 1 EACH)
___ Excedrin	3.35
___ Aspirin	1.35
___ Pain/Naproxen	2.60
___ Ibuprofen	2.55
___ Non Aspirin	2.00
___ A & D Ointment	2.50
___ Acne Treatment Cream	1.60
___ Hemorrhoid Cream	1.25
___ Tucks	4.85
___ Pepto-Bismol	2.40
___ Gas-X	3.20
___ Milk of Magnesia	2.25
___ Fiber (Orange Metamucil)	8.60
___ Lactose Relief	5.50
___ Laxative	1.50
___ Anti-Diarrheal	3.25
___ Culace	2.75
___ Antacid Chewable	2.50
___ Ranitidine	2.28
___ Muscle Rub	2.25
___ Cortizone Cream	1.80
___ Omeprazole	10.75
___ Antibiotic Cream	2.10
___ Dr. Sch. Gel Inserts	15.60
___ Comfort Insole	2.35
___ Tolfinate Foot Cream	1.45
___ Clotrimazole (Athletes foot)	2.20
___ Gold Bond Foot Powder	4.90
___ Foot Powder	1.50
___ Medicated Body Powder	1.25
___ Abreva	23.35
___ Eye Drops	2.50
___ Artificial Tears	3.30
___ Opcon Allergy Eye Drops	8.50
___ Nasal Spray-D	2.40
___ Saline Mist/Nasal	1.85
___ Nasacort Allergy Spray	19.95
___ Claritin	1.50
___ CTM's Allergy	1.30
___ Cough Syrup	2.45
___ Halls w/ Lemon	2.10
___ Halls Sugar Free	2.75
___ Chest Rub	2.10

VITAMINS (limit 1 each)
___ Advance Ultrex Plus	3.95
___ Vitamin B-Complex	2.95
___ Vitamin C	2.95
___ Calcium Tab	2.10

LIP CARE (limit 1 each)
___ Blistex Lip Ointment	1.80
___ Chapstick Lip Balm	2.00
___ Carmex Lip Balm	1.80

HEALTH FOODS (limit 10 each)
___ Honey & Oat Granola Bar	0.50
___ Sweet /Salty Almond Bar	0.65
___ P/B & Jelly Ultra Bar	1.55
___ Choco Caramel Ultra Bar	1.55
___ Cookies N Cream Ultra Bar	1.55
___ Rice Cakes	3.40
___ Oatmeal Varity	3.75 K
___ Oatmeal Plain	3.75 K
___ Honey Nut Granola BAG	3.00
___ Wheat Germ	3.15 K

CEREAL (limit 5 each)
___Honey & Oats Cereal	2.70
___Golden Puffs	3.05

CHIPS (limit 5 each)
___Tortillas Chips	2.05
___Sour Cream & Onion	1.60 KH
___Ripple Chips	1.60 KH
___Sea Salt Plantain Chips	1.90 K
___White Cheddar Popcorn	1.20
___Moon Lodge Pretzels	1.80

RICE/TORTILLA/PASTA (limit 10 each)
___Long Grain Rice	1.15
___Brown Rice	1.35 KH
___Cheese Rice	1.70
___Flour Tortillas	1.50 K
___Whole Wheat Tortilla	2.35
___Tomato Basil Tortilla	2.35
___Macaroni & Cheese	1.50
___Angel Hair Pasta	1.25
___Ziti	1.15
___Barilla Wheat Pasta	2.45

SNACKS (limit 4 each)
___Vanilla Pudding	2.40 K
___Chocolate Pudding	2.40 K
___Peanut Butter	2.95

KOSHER/HALAL
___Pasta w. Garden Vegetables	5.10 KH
___Stuffed Chicken,Rice/Mushroom	6.15 K
___Cheese Ravioli	5.10 K
___Eggplant Parm in Marinara	5.10 K
___Florentine Lasagna	5.10 KH
___Chicken & Black Beans	5.10 H
___Gefen Noodle Bag	.90 KH

SOUPS (limit 24 total)
___Hot n Spicy Vegetable (Bag)	0.25
___Ramen Chicken Soup (Bag)	0.25
___Chili Soup (Bag)	0.25
___Thai Noodle Soup (Bag)	0.65
___Shrimp Cup Soup	0.50
___Cheddar Cup Soup	0.50

PRODUCE (limit 4 each)
___Garlic Pickle	0.70 K
___Hot Pickle	0.70 K
___Jalapeno Pepper	1.95
___Green Olives	1.30
___Hot Pepper Mix	2.15
___Refried Beans	2.20 KH
___Chorizo Beans	2.05
___Kidney Beans	1.65
___Black Beans	1.30
___Mashed Potatoes	1.35 KH

CRACKERS (limit 2 each)
___Goya Crackers	2.55 K
___Snack Cracker (4pack)	3.20 KH
___Unsalted Saltine	2.60 K
___Cheese Crackers (Box)	2.80 K
___Graham Crackers	2.85 K

DAIRY (limit 15 total)
___Smoked Gouda Spread	1.85
___Velveeta Jalapeno Tub	1.80
___Velveeta Block Cheese	2.90
___Mozzarella Block	1.60
___Shredded Mozzarella Pack	1.00 H
___Provolone Block	1.80

CONDIMENTS/SPICES (limit 2 each)
___Extra Virgin Olive Oil	3.85
___Ketchup	1.85
___Mayonnaise	2.90 K
___Mustard	1.40 K
___Ranch Dressing	.60
___Sweet &Hot Sauce	1.80
___Soy Sauce	1.55
___Louisiana Hot Sauce	1.40 K
___Sriracha Hot Chili Sauce	2.80 K
___Chili Garlic Sauce	1.95
___Italian Pasta Sauce	.80
___Grated Italian Cheese	3.75
___Mrs. Dash Table Blend	3.60 K
___Mrs. Dash Original	3.35 K
___Salt & Pepper Shaker	2.35
___Sazon	1.60
___Goya Adobo	1.90
___Onion Powder	1.55 K
___Powder Garlic	2.05 K
___Veggie Flakes	1.35 K
___Curry Powder	.90 K
___Italian Seasoning	1.55 K
___Powered Chicken Bouillon	1.25
___Knorr Chicken Bouillon	3.55

COOKIES (limit 4 each)
___Vanilla Wafers	2.20 KH
___Animal Crackers	2.05 K
___Cocoa Cookie Bag	1.05 K
___Iced Oatmeal Cookies	2.45
___Chewy Chocolate Chips	2.10
___Vanilla Cream Cookies	1.65k
___Bear Claw	1.00
___Cheese Danish	1.10
___Red Velvet Cupcake	1.00
___Blueberry Toastems	1.65

NUTS (limit 10 each)
___Almonds	4.05
___Honey Roasted Peanuts	.80 KH
___Mixed Nuts	3.40 K
___Unsalted Peanuts	2.80 K
___Salted Peanuts	1.70
___Cashews	5.40 KH
___Sunflower Seeds	.50 K

CANDY (limit 20 total)
___Tootsie Pop Drops	1.40
___Peanut Butter Snickers	1.00
___Big Kit Kat	.95
___Dove Dark Chocolate Bar	1.05
___M&M's Peanut	1.05
___Hershey Kisses	1.95
___Vanilla Caramels	.65
___Peppermints	1.15
___Sugar Free Jolly Rancher	2.60
___Sugar Free Wild Fruit	.75
___Chocolate Peanut Clusters	1.55

MEATS/FISH
___Chicken Pouch	3.90
___Buffalo Chicken Bites	2.05
___Turkey Bites	2.05
___Pepperoni Slices	2.05
___Turkey & Swiss Stick	1.30
___Beef Summer Sausage	1.90
___Honey Pepper Turkey Stick	2.25
___Beef Stew Pouch	2.30
___Seasoned Ground Beef	3.25
___Hot Beef Summer Sausage	1.95
___Tuna	1.65 KH
___Mackerel	1.15 KH
___Albacore Tuna	2.25 K
___Yellow Fin Tuna	2.25 K
___Pink Salmon	2.70 K

MIXES/TEAS (limit 3 each)
___Gatorade Fruit Punch	2.15
___Polar Blast S/F	1.20
___Berry Bonkers S/F	1.20
___Diet Raspberry Snapple	1.20
___Diet Peach Snapple	1.20
___True Lemon	4.40 K
___True Lime	4.40 K
___Hot Tea Bags	2.60

COFFEE/COCOA (limit 3 each)
___Columbian Coffee	3.60 K
___Folgers Coffee	3.60 K
___Cappuccino French Vanilla	1.75 K
___Plain Creamer	2.15
___French Vanilla Creamer	3.40
___FV Bagged Creamer	1.40
___Decaffeinated Coffee	3.55 K
___Regular Cocoa (Bag)	1.80
___Espresso	1.95 KH
___Instant Milk (Box)	4.30 K
___Soy Milk	1.40 K
___Vanilla Almond Milk	1.75

SWEETENERS (limit 3 total)
___Splenda (box)	3.75
___Sweet & Low (box)	3.00 K
___Honey	2.85 K
___Stevia	2.15

SODA /DRINKS (limit 3 total)
___Coca Cola	5.15
___Diet Coca Cola	5.15
___Sprite	5.15
___Orange Vanilla Coca Cola	5.15
___Dasani Water	.60(24)

RELIGIOUS ITEMS
Must have signed cop-out by Religious Services
___Kufi Cap (Black)	6.89
___Kufi Cap (White)	5.69
___Prayer Oil	3.00
___Miswak Stick	0.70
___Prayer Rug	10.00

LOCKS (limit 1 total)
___Combination Lock	5.95

ELECTRONICS (limit 1 each)
___MP3 Player	88.90
___Clear Tunes Radio	23.00
___MP3 Play Cover	3.25
___MP3 Armband	7.75
___Koss Headphone	35.00
___JVC Earbuds	10.35
___Y Adapter	4.70
___Fan	19.50
___Book Light	9.75
___Alarm Clock	10.50
___Casio Men's Watch	50.00

BATTERIES (Limit 2 each)
___AA	1.45
___D Battery	2.55
___AAA	1.45
___Watch Battery	2.60

*Battery Number _____
*Battery Numbers not in stock sizes must be requested by cop-out.

RECREATION (limit 2 each)
___Playing Cards	2.60
___Pinochle Cards	1.70

BOOK/STATIONERY (limit 3 each)
___Phone Book	2.35(4)
___Photo Album	9.75(1)
___Photo Album Refills	4.75(2)
___Pencils (4-pk)	0.55(4)
___Envelope (Box)	1.80(4)
___Typewriter Ribbon	7.65(1)
___Envelope (Big/Yellow)	0.20(10)
___Bic Pen (2/pk)	1.10(4)
___Writing Pad	1.05(4)
___Notebook	1.70(4)
___Correction tape	9.60(4)
___Clear Legal Binders	1.95(10)
___Hobby Scissors	2.90(1)

EYEWEAR (limit 1 each)
___Reading Glasses	4.90-7.80
___Circle Size: 1.25- 1.75- 2.0- 2.25- 3.0	
___Ohana Sun Glasses	7.20
___Eyewear Retaining Cord	4.15

GREETING CARDS   0.55 Each
___KID / ADULT BIRTHDAY	
___LOVE YOU	
___SPANISH LOVE	
___FRIENDSHIP	
___SPANISH FRIENDSHIP	
___SYMPATHY	
___MISS YOU	
___THINKING OF YOU	
___THANK YOU	

ICE CREAM (limit 3 total)
See Selection at window
___Pints	2.65

HOLIDAY ITEMS
WHILE SUPPLIES LAST
YOGURT COVERED PRETZELS	1.45
BEANITOS BLACK BEAN CHIPS	3.00
TOSTITOS DIP	.90

[signature]
Approved
M. Licon-Vitale, Warden   4/8/19

[signature]
Approved
D. Womeldorf, Associate Warden

CHECK YOUR RECIPT BEFORE EXITING THE LOBBY – ONCE YOU LEAVE SALE IS FINAL.

NO RETURNS.

ALL PRICES ARE SUBJECT TO CHANGE WITHOUT NOTICE.

K = kosher
H = halal

Recipes from The MCC Kitchen

Mama Carmen's Recipes

"Hi, I am Carmen. I am fifty-eight years old. I have three adult children and five grandchildren. I am a certified home aide and a certified school bus attendant. I love to be active and exercise."

Mama Carmen, how we used to call her, was a short and energetic lady. She was always up to something—cooking, playing cards, cleaning, or talking about her kids. Regardless of what she was doing she had her headphones on and was dancing all the time.

Apple Juice

Ingredients
- Apples

Instructions
1. Put the apples in a box with lid.
2. Poke apples with a fork in several places.
3. Microwave for 3-5 min at a time.
4. Drain juice and microwave again until the apples are drained.
5. Toss apples or make puree.

Plantain and Pork Skin

Ingredients
- plantain chips
- pork skin (lemon/lime)
- seasonings: garlic, adobo

Instructions
1. Smash the plantain and pork skin.
2. Mix with seasonings and add water until a dough is formed.
3. Make patties and lay on a white sheet.
4. Microwave for approx 15 minutes, turning at least once.
5. Microwave more as per need and liking.

Cindy's Recipes

"Hi, I am Cindy, from California. I have two children. I love to experiment with food."

Salsa with Cheese and Sausage

Ingredients
- salsa (main line)
- cheese
- sausage

Instructions
1. Mix together.
2. Microwave approx. 3 minutes or until starts boiling.

Honey Mustard Salad Dressing

Ingredients
- mustard
- honey
- ketchup
- mayo
- chipotle cheese

- salsa (main line)
- bag of The Whole Shabang or chips

Instructions
1. Mix together.

Sushi

Ingredients
- mackerel
- oysters
- clams
- yellow tuna
- sardines
- Sazón
- garlic
- mayo
- chipotle seasoning
- yellow cheddar cheese (optional)
- rice
- oatmeal
- salt
- water
- soy
- mustard
- ketchup
- honey or sugar

Instructions
1. Mix rice with oatmeal, salt, garlic, and water.
2. Let sit for at least 1 hour.
3. Sauce: mix soy with mayo, mustard, ketchup, and honey, and cook until boiling.
4. Spread the rice on a plastic bag and put the mixed fish with seasonings in the middle, then roll.
5. Enjoy with sauce!

Evelyn's Recipes

Evelyn was a young, beautiful Hispanic lady. She had long dark hair that she always kept nicely done. She was a hairdresser by trade and helped ladies at MCC look as decent as possible under the circumstances. Like every other Hispanic that I met she cooked insanely well. She had two young children. I met them and her family in visiting.

She was one of the first people I met. When I got to MCC I had long red nails, as I've always worn. Evelyn was appointed by the unit secretary, yes, the same one from Part I of the book, to help me cut them off and remove the polish. Obviously, we had no acetone and no cuticle nippers or files. They only had some very small nail clippers. Evelyn was nice enough to lend me her nail clipper and helped me cut my nails short and peel off the gel.

Paella by Evelyn
For 8 people

Ingredients
- 3 packets of clams
- 3 packets of oysters
- 3 packets of mackerel
- garlic, salt, pepper, Sazón
- 2 cans of V8
- corn or mixed vegetables (optional)
- 3 rice bags

Instructions
1. Cook fish.
2. Add rice (cooked separately).
3. Add the seasoning and cook together for 5-6 minutes.
4. Note: Any fish or combination.

Mackerel Soup
Ingredients
- Bag of vegetables

- V8
- mackerel (based on number of people)
- seasonings
- vegetable noodle soup (a little, not the entire pack)

Instructions
1. Mix and microwave for 8 minutes.

Judy's Recipes

"My name is Judy. I am forty-two years old. I have three natural children and three adopted me as their mother. I also have eight grandchildren. I love playing handball and crocheting."
Judy crocheted exquisite pieces. She made my daughter a bathing suit for her birthday.

Taco Bowl

For 12 people

Ingredients
- 4 sausage
- 3 Spam
- 4 rice bags (any type)
- 2 chicken
- 2 mackerel
- beans (optional)
- tortilla large
- 5 different cheeses (jalapeño, chipotle, mozzarella, Laughing Cow, cheese from the mac and cheese)
- milk
- seasonings (Sazón, garlic, salt, pepper)

Instructions
1. Cut pieces and cook each meat separately 2-3 min.
2. Sauce on top: 3 Laughing Cow plus 2 packets of powder cheese from the mac and cheese mix with milk melted into a cream.
3. Put tortilla into a bowl, put 6-7 spoons of rice on the bottom, put the meat and fish per desire, cheeses per desire, cheese cream, and any sauce you want on top (optional).
4. Microwave for 1.5 minutes to get crispy.

Mofongo

Same ingredients and directions as the Taco Bowl above. Just replace tacos with plantain chips.

Mamacita's Kitchen

Mamacita was a super funny character. She was an older woman who was always cooking and taking care of somebody. At some point she was moved to the cell next to us. She had her headphones on with music blasting and sang until she would fall asleep, which was closer to midnight. People from the other cells were yelling, cursing, and screaming at her to shut up. The last resort was for the officer to unlock her cell and make her stop.

Cake

Ingredients
- any cookies preferable chocolate cookies. If plain cookies add some peanut butter
- 1/2 pint of milk or ginger ale
- creamer
- 1/2 packet hot chocolate powder
- either chocolate or punch (for color)

Instructions
1. In a box with lid, crush cookies and add milk or ginger ale.
2. Microwave for 5 minutes.
3. Let cool and turn over on a sheet or plate.
4. Frosting: add creamer, hot chocolate, and chocolate or punch.
5. Pour over the cake.

Pepsi Rice

Ingredients
- rice
- Pepsi
- soy sauce
- honey
- noodles from any soup
- meat 2-3 kinds

- mayo
- envelope (letter size or bigger)

Instructions

1. Mix rice and noodles with mayo.
2. Place in an envelope.
3. Microwave until crispy or golden.
4. Add meats, honey, soy, seasonings (adobe, Sazón).
5. Microwave for 3 minutes.
6. Put rice and noodles on top and then pour the Pepsi on top (almost one full can).
7. Cover and microwave for 6 minutes, stir, then microwave for another 2 minutes.

Hot Rice

Ingredients

- refried beans or pinto beans
- salsa hot
- meats

Instructions

1. Cook meats separately.
2. Mix meats with rice and microwave for 3 minutes, stir, then microwave for another 3 minutes.
3. Serve with the beans (cooked separately) and salsa.

Potato Log or Tamales (just add cheese)

Ingredients

- nachos or The Whole Shebangs
- water
- tuna
- mackerel
- sausage
- cheese
- plastic bag

Instructions

1. Crush the chips, mix with water, and make a dough.
2. Spread it on a plastic bag.
3. Cook the ingredients separately and then put it on the dough.
4. Wrap it and microwave it for 10 minutes.

Sushi Roll with Sauce

Ingredients

- rice
- oatmeal
- seasoning
- plastic bag
- mackerel
- tuna
- cheese (optional)

Instructions

1. Mix rice and oatmeal, salt and pepper and water and let sit for 5 minutes.
2. Put on a plastic bag flat, then add the fish cooked separately.
3. Roll and enjoy!

Sushi Sauce

Ingredients

- 2 spoons honey
- 2 spoons soy sauce
- 2-3 packs mustard
- mayo
- Sazón
- garlic

Instructions

1. Mix all ingredients.
2. Microwave for 15 seconds.

Salad Dressing

Ingredients
- ketchup
- mustard
- mayo
- honey
- seasonings (adobo, Sazón, garlic, salt/pepper)

Instructions
1. Mix together.

Chicken Spread

Ingredients
- shredded chicken (main line)
- mustard
- ketchup
- mayo
- Laughing Cow cheese
- seasonings (Sazón, honey)

Instructions
1. Mix together.
2. Microwave for 15 seconds.

Tortilla Wrap

Ingredients
- tortilla
- tuna
- The Whole Shebangs chips
- sugar or honey
- mayo
- Laughing Cow cheese

Instructions
1. Mix and wrap.

Dumplings

Ingredients

- tortilla (small main line)
- creamer
- cheese
- meat (any)
- milk

Instructions

1. Mix the creamer with milk and/or tortilla and make a paste or dough.
2. Fill it with meat and microwave for 5 minutes.

Chicken / Mackerel Patties by Carolina and Mamacita

Ingredients

- saltine crackers or Ritz crackers
- mackerel or chicken or tuna or salmon
- seasoning: garlic, Sazón
- mayo
- honey (optional)

Instructions

1. Crush the crackers.
2. Mix with the fish or chicken and seasonings.
3. Make small patties and line them up on a sheet or cardboard.
4. Microwave for 3 minutes.
5. Carolina adds honey, both saltine and Ritz and microwaves for longer.

Com Com by Carolina and Mamacita

Ingredients

- Vienna sausage
- yellow rice
- seasoning
- V8
- beans

Instructions

1. Microwave the rice for 5 minutes until crunchy.
2. Cook the sausage and beans separately with seasoning and V8.
3. Then mix with the rice.

Marie's Recipes

"I'm Marie. I'm 37 years old from Elizaville, NY. I have two children—three and six years old. My hobbies are reading, basketball, softball, and caring for people. I am a nurse and caregiver by profession."

These are Marie's recipe's from when she was in MCC.

Marie's Chicken Roll

Ingredients

- The Whole Shebangs chips
- chicken, any meat or fish
- cheese

Instructions

1. Crush The Whole Shebangs, add water, and make a dough.
2. Season meat and cook for 1-2 minutes.
3. In a plastic bag add the dough and all ingredients (meat and cheese).
4. Roll and tie the ends.
5. Microwave for 5 minutes.

Tuna Wrap

Ingredients

- tortilla or The Whole Shebangs chips
- tuna
- spices (optional)
- sugar (optional)

Instructions

1. Mix the tuna with the spices.
2. Enjoy with tortilla or The Whole Shebangs chips.

Macaroni Salad

Ingredients

- macaroni from mac and cheese
- tuna
- mayo
- garlic
- Sazón
- salt

Instructions

1. Cook the macaroni.
2. Add the rest and mix.

Enjoy!

Sharon's Recipes

"Hi, I'm Sharon. It is a fun thing to make cakes for people!
I would do more with fruits but people like the chocolate and
they ask me to make it all the time."

Ms. Sharon was an older African American woman who worked
in laundry, but her main occupation was making cakes. When she
wasn't in the laundromat, she was in the kitchen making a cake.

Ms. Sharon's Cheesecake

Ingredients

- 2-3 bars Snickers or Almond Joy
- 2 round boxes Laughing Cow cheese
- 1 pack graham crackers
- 10 sleeves butter
- French vanilla creamer
- regular creamer
- sugar
- any chocolate
- a pinch of lemon Kool-Aid

Instructions

1. Bottom part is made of half of the crushed crackers mixed with half of the butter.
2. Mix cream cheese and sugar, then the rest of butter and mix well.
3. Add the pinch of lemon Kool-Aid.
4. Melt chocolate, mix it with Snickers or Almond Joy.
5. Put cream on top of the crackers.
6. Sprinkle crushed crackers and another melted Snickers or Almond Joy on top.
7. Keep in ice for at least 3 hours to cool down.

Note: Butter sleeves are provided during breakfast service. Each sleeve contains approximately half an ounce, equivalent to a standard serving size, which is typically considered as one serving. It's worth noting that while it is referred to as "butter," I believe it is actually margarine.

Nancy's Recipes

"I am Nancy. I am an educator. I have 5 children.
I came to the US believing in the American dream.
I love to dance and play soccer."

Noodles and Sausage

Ingredients

- sausage
- rice
- noodles
- seasonings (garlic, chipotle)

Instructions

1. Fry sausage separately in garlic powder and chipotle seasoning for 2 minutes or until color change (stir occasionally).
2. In a separate bowl, boil the noodles until halfway tender.
3. In a separate bowl, mix the dry rice with some Sazón.
4. Pour the dry rice into the bowl that has the fried sausage, stir, and mix.
5. Add the noodles with the water and cook for 4 minutes or until the ingredients are cooked.

Sweet Grits or Farina

Ingredients

- 4 oz dry grits
- 1 carton milk
- 8 oz creamer
- 10 packs sugar
- 1 pinch of salt

Instructions

1. Mix the grits in hot water and let stand for 2-4 minutes, then add more hot water until it's watery.
2. Microwave for 4 minutes, remove occasionally to stir (make

sure it is not too hard).

3. As you are stirring, add the milk and beat it like eggs.
4. Put back in microwave for 3 minutes and watch it so it does not overflow.
5. Add the creamer and sugar, put back in microwave for 3-4 minutes, stir occasionally.
6. Cook time 10-15 minutes.

Rita's Recipes

"Hi, I'm Rita from Hong Kong."

One of Rita's recipes led to an unexpected incident during our time at MCC. Initially, she monopolized the microwave for extended periods, refusing others the opportunity to use it until she was finished. However, she eventually learned a valuable lesson about the microwave dynamics.

One morning, while preparing a dish, Rita had set the microwave timer to its maximum limit of 5 minutes. A typically kind morning officer, despite his general affability, grew increasingly frustrated when he politely asked Rita to pause the microwave briefly so he could heat his coffee. When she declined, insisting he wait, he reached his breaking point and unplugged the microwave, effectively removing it from the kitchen. This action led to all of us being placed in lockdown for the remainder of the day and Rita taken to the SHU for a week. To have the microwave reinstated in our unit, we had to seek approval from the unit manager, a process that took nearly a week to complete.

Tamales

Ingredients
- Doritos
- hot chips
- chicken
- sausage (optional)

- refried beans
- cheese bottle
- mozzarella cheese

Instructions
1. Crush Doritos and hot chips and mix with water to make a dough.
2. Lay on a plastic bag. Cook the meats separate from the beans.
3. Add the meats and cheese on top of the dough. Fold it.
4. Add shredded mozzarella on top.
5. Microwave for 10 minutes.

Vegetarian Noodle Soup

Ingredients
- noodle soup
- eggs
- lettuce

Instructions
1. Mix all together.
2. Cook for 2-3 minutes.

Sushi Roll

Ingredients
- 2 pks rice
- 3 bag tuna
- salt and pepper
- soy sauce
- hot sauce
- sugar
- peanuts

Instructions

1. Cook rice not too soft, lay on plastic, let cool.
2. 2 packs of rice and 3 bags of tuna make 20 rolls.
3. Mix tuna with salt and pepper, soy sauce and add rice.
4. Take 2 piece of cardboard to help fold the rice to stay square.

Wasabi Sauce

Ingredients

- hot sauce
- soy sauce
- sugar
- crushed peanuts

Instructions

1. Mix hot sauce with soy sauce and a tiny bit of sugar.
2. Sprinkle crushed peanuts on top to resemble sesame seeds.

Zoraida's Recipes

"I am Zoraida. I am a fifty-year-old single mother. I love to crochet because it is very relaxing and therapeutic. It transports my mind to my family and/or to the person I am crocheting for. I am crocheting for loved ones to let them know they are in my thoughts or just as a token of appreciation. Besides, the time goes faster. I invite everybody to pick up a skein of yarn and a crochet hook and give it a try!"

Zoraida's animal farm

At some point she had a full farm of stuffed animals made by her crochet, creativity, and talent.

Fish and Grits

Ingredients

- grits
- butter
- 1 bag mackerel

- seasonings
- Velveeta cheese

Instructions
1. Season grits to taste, add butter, cook for about 3 minutes.
2. Check and stir, add more water if needed.
3. Add cheese and cook for another 2 minutes.
4. Check and stir, and add the mackerel, cook for another 1 minute.

Banana Oatmeal

Ingredients
- oatmeal
- 6oz water
- 1 banana
- 1 milk
- cinnamon, sugar, or French vanilla

Instructions
1. Add water to one pack of oatmeal, slice banana, and smash with a fork until all mixed up.
2. Heat a container of milk for 1 minute and add to oatmeal, then heat up for 1 more minute.
3. Season to taste.

Enjoy!

Rita's Recipes

Rita, my savior, without words…literally

"I am Rita Gina, forty years old from Mexico. I have two adult children who are eighteen and twenty-two. I love to spend time with my family, cooking and entertaining people. I am a podologist by profession."

Despite the language barrier between Rita, who didn't speak a word of English, and me, who couldn't communicate in Spanish, we managed to develop a unique culinary language that became our daily means of expression. Rita consistently looked out for Rose and me, ensuring we never missed a meal. On weekends, we gathered in the kitchen, often with the Spanish TV playing in the background. It was amusing how I always found my name on the schedule for certain telenovelas that Rita was avidly following.

As my time at MCC drew to a close, I had earned the respect of both inmates and officers to the extent that nobody dared to approach me with any complaints or issues. Rita would be engrossed in her favorite shows while skillfully preparing our meals, and I would watch her with admiration, silently taking notes on her cooking techniques and secret recipes.

Chicharrón Salsa

Ingredients
- salsa (main line) tomato sauce, cilantro, onion
- 1 bottle picante sauce
- chipotle seasoning
- 2 cans of V8 juice
- salt and pepper
- water 325 ml
- 3 bg pork skin
- 1 bg refried beans precooked
- 1 mozzarella bar
- jalapeño beans

Instructions
1. Cook salsa, picante sauce, chipotle seasoning, V8, salt/pepper, water for 2-3 minutes, put in the beans, then cook another 2 minutes.
2. Add the chicharrón, then cook for another 2-4 minutes until it is not too soft and not too hard.

Pasta Alfredo with Tuna

Ingredients
- soup (any kind)
- 2 pieces Laughing Cow cheese
- tuna
- seasonings (Sazón, salt/pepper)

Instructions
1. Boil noodles and toss the liquid.
2. Add 2 Laughing Cow, seasoning, and tuna and mix.

Mole

Ingredients
- chicken (main line)
- 1/2 pack sunflower seeds
- 1/2 pack peanuts
- 6 spoons hot chocolate powder
- spicy sauce (picante)
- chipotle powder
- salt/pepper

Instructions
1. Crush sunflower seeds and peanuts.
2. Mix with water and make a paste, then add everything else. Add hot water and make a more liquid paste. Microwave for 3 minutes.
3. Add shredded chicken. Mix and microwave for 2 minutes.
4. Eat with tortilla and beans and rice on the side.

Tacos

Ingredients
- beans
- beef sausage
- chipotle cheese
- 1/2 bottle Sazón

- large tortilla
- water
- salsa
- fresh cheese

Instructions
1. Cut beef sausage and microwave until crispy, 2-3 minutes in microwave.
2. Add water, beans, cheese, and Sazón.
3. Cut large tortilla into 4 pieces.
4. Put beans onto tortilla and microwave for max 1 minute.

Fish Soup - Mexican

Ingredients
- 1 pack of vegetables
- 1 pack of corn
- 3 cans of V8
- 2 packs vegetable soup seasonings
- Sazón, chipotle powder, salt/pepper

Instructions
1. Mix the vegetables, corn, V8, and seasonings, and cook for 2 minutes.
2. In another bowl, cook the vegetable soups including the powder for 3 minutes.
3. Add the soup to the vegetables, mix and cook together for another 2 minutes.

Potato Salad

Ingredients
- potato main line (peeled)
- eggs (main line) (no yolk)
- mayo
- BBQ sauce
- pepper
- tuna (optional)

Instructions
1. Cut the potatoes and egg whites in small cubes, mix togeth-er with mayo and spices, and cook for 1 minute.
2. Eat with crackers.

Chicken Tacos

Ingredients
- chicken stew (main line)
- 1 bar chipotle cheese
- 5 pieces Laughing cow cheese
- bottle cheddar cheese
- milk
- tacos (main line)

Instructions
1. Mix the Laughing Cow with the yellow cheddar cheese (about 2 spoons) and milk. Microwave for 1 minute, then add the chipotle cheese and cook for another 1 minute.
2. Break the tacos into small pieces and add to salsa (our own, see below) and microwave for 2 minutes.
3. In a bowl put the salsa, the cheese, and add the chicken.

Salsa (our own)

Ingredients
- 3 cans of V8
- pepper
- 1/2 bottle picante sauce
- chipotle powder

Instructions
1. Mix and microwave for 3 minutes.

Chinese Rice

Ingredients

- hot beef sausage
- mixed vegetables
- soy sauce
- rice

Instructions

1. Cut up and cook the sausage for 2 minutes.
2. Drain oil out, add rice and water, mix and cook for 3 minutes.
3. Add veggies and soy sauce and cook for another 2 minutes.

Note: The girls have been making fresh cheese almost every weekend. I've always found it perplexing why creating fresh cheese would be classified as contraband, particularly given its straightforward preparation and the easy accessibility of all the ingredients required. To protect those engaged in its production, the recipe has intentionally been left unattributed to any specific person.

Fresh Cheese

Ingredients

- 8 8oz milk boxes (from breakfast)
- 1/4 cup vinegar
- salt to taste

Instructions

1. Pour all of the milk into a large container and microwave for two minutes stirring occasionally.
2. Stirr in the vinegar. Let sit for 10 minutes.
3. Add the salt.
4. Strain it through a cheese cloth, thin towel or a clean t-shirt. Let it drip for couple of hours.
5. Remove the cloth.

My Recipes From Prison

Fruit Salad

Ingredients

- any fruits served at main line
- granola bar
- honey
- walnuts or any nuts (optional)

Instructions

1. Cut fruit to the desired size.
2. Crush granola.
3. Mix with honey and nuts.

Biscuit Salami: Turkish Delight, Tea Biscuits, and Chocolate

Ingredients

- 4-5 cubes Turkish delight
- 1 pack tea biscuits
- chocolate of choice
- walnuts or any nuts of preference

Instructions

1. Chop the Turkish delight into small pieces.
2. Melt the chocolate in a bowl placed in hot water.

3. Crush the tea biscuits and incorporate with the rest of the ingredients.
4. Crush walnuts and spread on top.
5. You can actually roll it into a salami.
6. I kept it in a small, covered container on ice, since I didn't have a fridge.

Banana and Chocolate Dessert

Ingredients
- 1 matzo sheet
- 1 banana
- melted chocolate

Instructions
1. Spread the melted chocolate on the matzo sheet.
2. Cut the banana in small pieces and place on top.

Breakfast of Champions

Ingredients
- oatmeal
- banana (or any fresh fruit)
- chocolate
- dates
- almonds

Instructions
1. Mix the oatmeal (from main line) with the fruit and choco-late.
2. Serve with dates filled with almonds.

Note: Dates were only available to the Muslim population, along with Turkish delight and sometimes (very rarely) peach puree and fig cookies only during Ramadan. I had friends who were registered as Muslims and had access to those products. We bought for each other things we needed in the same amount. The same with the matzo or coconut macaroons with the Jewish ladies during Passover.

Tuna Salad

Ingredients

- tuna
- cucumber
- pickle
- mayo
- sunflower seeds
- spices

Instructions

1. Drain the pack of tuna.
2. Chop the cucumber and pickle.
3. Mix together with the mayo, sunflower seeds, and spices of choice.

Mofongo

Ingredients

- 1 bag of salty plantain chips (green bag). You can use the sweet ones, (the yellow bag) if you can't find the salty
- 1 block of mozzarella or provolone—you can use Velveeta if you don't have any other cheese
- spices: whatever you like
- meat or fish: whatever you like, you can even use pork skin. I used 1 mackerel pouch

This quantity was way too much for me to eat at one time so I would always share it with someone.

Instructions

1. Crush the plantains.
2. Add the cheese.
3. Cook in bag, in hot water, until the cheese is melted.
4. Add the other ingredients and mix well.
5. Serve hot!

www.ingramcontent.com/pod-product-compliance
Lightning Source LLC
Chambersburg PA
CBHW071158130626
46553CB00004B/1705